TANDEM

Sullivan's I.Q. Tests

Also by Norman Sullivan in
Tandem editions

SULLIVAN'S FIRST BOOK OF CROSSWORD PUZZLES
SULLIVAN'S SECOND BOOK OF CROSSWORD PUZZLES
SULLIVAN'S THIRD BOOK OF CROSSWORD PUZZLES
SULLIVAN'S FOURTH BOOK OF CROSSWORD PUZZLES
SULLIVAN'S FIFTH BOOK OF CROSSWORD PUZZLES
SULLIVAN'S SIXTH BOOK OF CROSSWORD PUZZLES
SULLIVAN'S SEVENTH BOOK OF CROSSWORD PUZZLES

Sullivan's I.Q. Tests

Norman Sullivan

TANDEM

First published in Great Britain by
Tandem Publishing Ltd, 1976

Tandem Books are published by Tandem Publishing Ltd,
14 Gloucester Road, London SW7
A Howard & Wyndham Company

Made and printed in Great Britain by
Hunt Barnard Printing Ltd, Aylesbury, Bucks.

Contents

Introduction 7

Group 1 Not Difficult 15

Tests 1–5 16

Answers 55

Ratings 68

Group 11 Fairly Difficult 71

Tests 6–10 72

Answers 115

Ratings 134

Group 111 Difficult 137

Tests 11–14 138

Answers 171

Ratings 188

Introduction

What *is* 'intelligence?' We talk of a dog as being '*so* intelligent'. What we really mean is that it obeys us *because it understands what we say*. Is this, then, a clue as to what intelligence is – the ability to *understand*?

Volumes have been written endeavouring to define what it is. In some of them the human brain is dissected in words and diagrams, many of which are so complicated, so interwoven with arrows leading to obscure footnotes, that merely to understand them would presuppose a degree of intelligence almost equal to that of the writer of the book.

If, then, it is so difficult to offer an explanation as to what 'intelligence' really is, how much more difficult it must be to have the temerity to set a 'quotient' on it.

An 'I.Q. Test' is designed to measure the 'Intelligence Quotient' of those undergoing it.

In setting such a test it is surely necessary to try to draw a fine line of distinction between education, experience, age, aptitude – and a 'quiz temperament'.

It is worth considering each of these in greater detail.

(1) EDUCATION.

It is generally accepted that education in itself has little or no bearing on intelligence. In the main this is true, and certainly much would depend upon the course which the education followed.

Perhaps 'common sense' is a close definition of 'intelligence'. Because a person has been educated it by no means implies that he has common sense. Education could teach him how to find the area of an irregular shape; how to recognise a Greek poet by the style of verse; to recite the names of mythical characters with the fluency that lesser mortals would recite the letters of the alphabet.

In higher education a student may be 'reading' English Literature, Sociology, Classical History, or whatever the choice is, and it is fair to assume that if one's education and study were directed into one single channel almost exclusively for a long period of time one would become reasonably expert in the subject.

Yet that same person might find himself completely floored if posed the simple problem: If a drawer contained many stockings thrown in at random and the stockings were of three different colours, what is the least number of stockings one would have to select in the dark to be sure of getting a matching pair? – a question that someone completely lacking in education might answer without hesitation.

Education, in its broadest sense, must surely be a useful and undeniable asset to the acquisition of intelligence, but if of a purely specialised nature could have the opposite effect, in making the recipient completely expert at answering questions on his chosen subject, yet quite abysmally ignorant of ordinary mundane subjects.

When, for example, a well-educated person learns to drive a car he often takes much longer than one whose education was scant. Driving instructors usually maintain that it is easier to teach a person who can barely read or write than one who follows a profession, such as a doctor or a schoolteacher. The main asset in learning to drive is common sense, and 'road sense' (which is merely common sense as applied to traffic and road conditions) is something which the finest instructor in the world cannot teach.

So we are faced with the problem: Does *knowledge*, whether of a specialized nature or of a general nature, in itself inspire intelligence?

(2) EXPERIENCE.

'Experientia docet,' said the Romans, which, as any educated (sic) person will know, means 'experience teaches'. The more experience (or practice) that a person has at a given task, the better will he become at performing it.

A regular solver of cryptic crossword puzzles will eventually know *from experience* what the compiler has in mind, especially if he specialises in one compiler's puzzles, though he is no more intelligent after working on the same puzzles for a year than he was a year ago. A crossword addict can often glance at an involved clue, recognise immediately that it contains an anagram, and frequently solve it in an instant, without even having to put pen to paper, in spite of the fact that the anagram may consist of fifteen letters.

Granted, then, that experience is an asset in this field, and the more diversified the experience the greater will be the ability to 'understand' – then the next factor to be considered – age – must be of some comparable importance.

(3) AGE.

It would be foolish and rash to claim that age improves intelligence, especially if dotage and senile decay are taken into account.

But obviously, experience is most likely to be increased with age, and an intelligent person may well draw on his experience to point guide-lines when trying to distinguish right from wrong.

Success at answering some questions posed in quiz programmes may depend on a knowledge of what has gone before. If a person is required to name a character or an event which featured in his own lifetime, then obviously he is more likely to be able to give an answer from *personal recollection* than one who has had to assimilate the fact by learning by rote. As an example of this, events which were in the news as recently as during the last war (1939–45) are easily brought to mind by people who are old enough to have played a part, either actively or passively, in those events than young people who were not even born, and to whom names like Eisenhower, Tedder, Ribbentrop, etc., mean no more than names learned from history books. General Alexander is only a name to them, probably meaning no more and no less than Alexander the Great.

Again, events in an ever-changing world – changes of names of countries; changes of governments and leaders; industrial changes – can often be traced back clearly in the memory of older persons who may have lived through many reigns and had first-hand experience of events which to others are merely boring items in a history book.

Shakespeare put it:

> 'Though age from folly could not give me freedom,
> It does from childishness.'

(4) APTITUDE.

'Aptitude Tests' are – or should be – an entirely different proposition from 'Intelligence Tests'.

If a firm requires to recruit a new employee and wants to assess his potential (his relative aptitude for the work he will have to do) a test *especially designed* to assist in making their decision can prove invaluable.

To give examples: if a business depended on the ability to distinguish colours accurately and instantly, and bearing in mind that a surprising number of people are colour-blind to a greater or lesser degree, then it is reasonable to subject a potential employee to a test devised to ascertain his colour-awareness; such a test could save many later recriminations by both employer and employee. If a firm required a filing clerk of a very specialized nature it is fair to accept that a test designed to ascertain whether the applicant could recognise matching shapes and patterns without undue delay would be a useful pointer; such a test might well prove the possession of an 'alphabetic mind', that is, the ability to place things in sequence (not necessarily alphabetic) without hesitation.

Aptitude, according to the dictionary, means 'fitness and ability'. Whether this is a sign of intelligence or whether it implies that a person possessing it is suitable for one particular type of job, may be a moot point, but is certainly worth assessing by a firm willing to pay money to one who has it.

Again, aptitude might be shown by a person completely *en rapport* with a particular subject, but conspicuously lacking in anything else.

A *general* aptitude, that is, a quickness for acquiring the know-how of a subject for which a person has no particular flair, must surely be largely dependent on 'intelligence': an ability to adapt oneself and to apply logic and reasoning to any given subject.

(5) 'QUIZ TEMPERAMENT.'

One of the most popular types of television programme is the quiz, and whatever its nature it always commands tremendous interest from the viewing public, who like to match their wits against the person being interrogated or against the panel of experts.

Although many of these quizzes, especially those using a panel of experts, are often of a highly specialized nature and the viewer can only marvel at the erudition of those answering the questions so fluently (usually having not the slightest inkling himself as to what the answer is) he nevertheless derives immense satisfaction on the rare occasions when he *is* able to supply an answer which has stumped the experts.

When the questions are not too difficult, such as when a single person is being asked questions on general knowledge, the viewer is often able to supply an answer which confounds the contestant. On these occasions he is apt to think: 'Fancy him not knowing the answer to *that* simple question! I knew it immediately,' overlooking the fact that any question is easy if you know the answer, though impossibly difficult if you do not, and have to rely on a random guess. (And television cameras have a great facility for blanking out the memory, even when you *do* know the answer.)

When you watch these programmes, do you envy those taking part and wish you were in their place, or do you feel sorry for them?

How do *you* fare in these quizzes? Do you frequently 'beat the panel', or are you always left aghast at their knowledge of the subject and ashamed of your own ignorance of it?

If the latter is the case, ask yourself: is it because they are more educated? (perhaps); older? (perhaps); more experienced? (perhaps); or more *intelligent*? (Surely not!) So, when it comes to answering questions in a quiz, 'intelligence' must come a very poor second to any of the other attributes.

My own personal definition of 'intelligence' is: the ability to reason in a rational and logical way and, from that reasoning, to gain understanding.

Some people have a *quick* reasoning ability, which makes them able participants in a quiz, especially when the winner is 'first on the button'; in the same way, some have an innate aptitude for examinations of any kind, even revelling in the challenge which they offer, while others almost petrify at the very thought of a test, which seems to drive all knowledge of the subject immediately from their mind. This 'quiz temperament' is akin to 'test match temperament'. Some cricketers can perform with consummate skill for their county, yet lack that vital 'test match temperament' which perpetually relegates them to non-selection for their country.

No discussion on intelligence could omit the importance of the effects of heredity and environment.

Many respected writers on the psychology of learning and factors influencing intelligence have carried out long and careful experiments on the subject, and it has been convincingly established that heredity has a marked effect on intelligence. In other words, intelligence is an inherited characteristic. But the hereditary influence is rapidly superseded by the effects of environment. Thus, a child born of highly intelligent parents is likely itself to be highly intelligent – PROVIDED THAT THE CHILD'S LATER ENVIRONMENT IS NOT SUCH AS WILL ADUMBRATE THE INHERITED FORCE. If the child is brought up in 'intellectual' surroundings its inherent intelligence is likely to develop and improve; but if it is brought up in a low-intellectual environment, in which little stimulus is offered to the development of logical thought and understanding, the advantage of heredity will be seriously diminished.

With all this said, I will avoid further dogmatism on the subject and, in offering this book, suggest that we say together: 'Shucks with "intelligence". Let's have some fun together and see how we rate with ourselves. Why should we try to measure out I.Q. against others, anyway?'

As this book is for readers of all ages and aptitudes, and I make no claim that it can give even a feasible assessment of the reader's I.Q., I merely express the hope that you will enjoy trying to unravel its mysteries.

There are too many imponderables to consider. If a 12-year-old could complete one of the fourteen tests and leave an adult at the post, I suppose he could claim a pretty high I.Q. But only *by comparison*, surely. Perhaps the 12-year-old was of 'average' intelligence and the adult was very much below 'average'.

Also worth considering is the time factor. If a person can give the correct answer to a problem in ten seconds he obviously merits more highly than one who takes thirty seconds to reach the answer. On the other hand, a person who gives a correct answer in thirty seconds is to be commended more highly than one who gives an *incorrect* answer in ten seconds.

HOW TO TACKLE

There are two ways in which you can benefit from and enjoy this book:

If you wish you can just work your way through it, enjoying (I hope) trying to answer the problems.

A better way is to start off with paper and pencil at the ready and, taking one test at a time, write down your answers. At the beginning of each test I suggest a time limit. Take the time when you start and finish *as soon as the time limit has expired*, regardless of any questions you have not tackled.

Then turn to the solutions at the back and assess your score (points are awarded for each answer).

Of course, after the time limit you could continue to try the questions that you didn't get down to before, but do not credit your score with these.

At the end of the *first group* of tests (there are five tests in Group I, five in Group II and four in Group III) find your total for the whole group and then assess your rating from the ratings given at the back of the book.

Two things I can guarantee: if you conscientiously attempt the tests, even if you don't do well at them, they will provide a useful foundation for I.Q. tests which you may take, either voluntarily or compulsorily, later on; and if you work your way through the book you will find that the experience you gain from the early (and easier) tests will help you a great deal when you tackle the later ones.

Throughout these tests I have endeavoured to strike a reasonable balance between Reasoning and Deduction, Vocabulary, Numerical skill, Knowledge, Visuo-spatial ability and Visual Perception. In fact the overall mixture is as follows:

Vocabulary	31%
Reasoning and deduction ..	28%
Numerical skill	17%
Knowledge	11%
Visuo-spatial ability	10%
Visual perception	3%

If, therefore, you compare your scores for ALL the tests with the total possible score shown in the ratings at the back of the book, you may be able to draw an inference as to which of those abilities are your strongest and weakest points.

Now! Paper and pencil ready? Look at your watch!
Five . . . four . . . three . . . two . . . one . . . GO!
And good luck!

NORMAN SULLIVAN

GROUP I

TESTS 1–5

Not Difficult

Vocabulary	30%
Visuo-spatial	19%
Numerical	17%
Reasoning and deduction	17%
Knowledge	10%
Visual perception	7%

TEST No. 1

(Time limit: 15 minutes)

1. Which is the intruder?

(a) VIXEN
(b) HEN
(c) PEACOCK
(d) FILLY
(e) MARE

2. Which one is wrong?

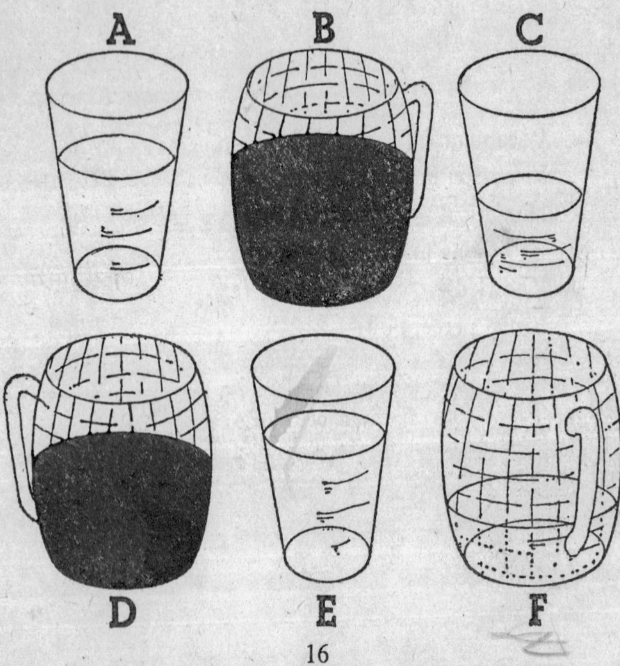

3. Which of the numbered shapes belongs to E?

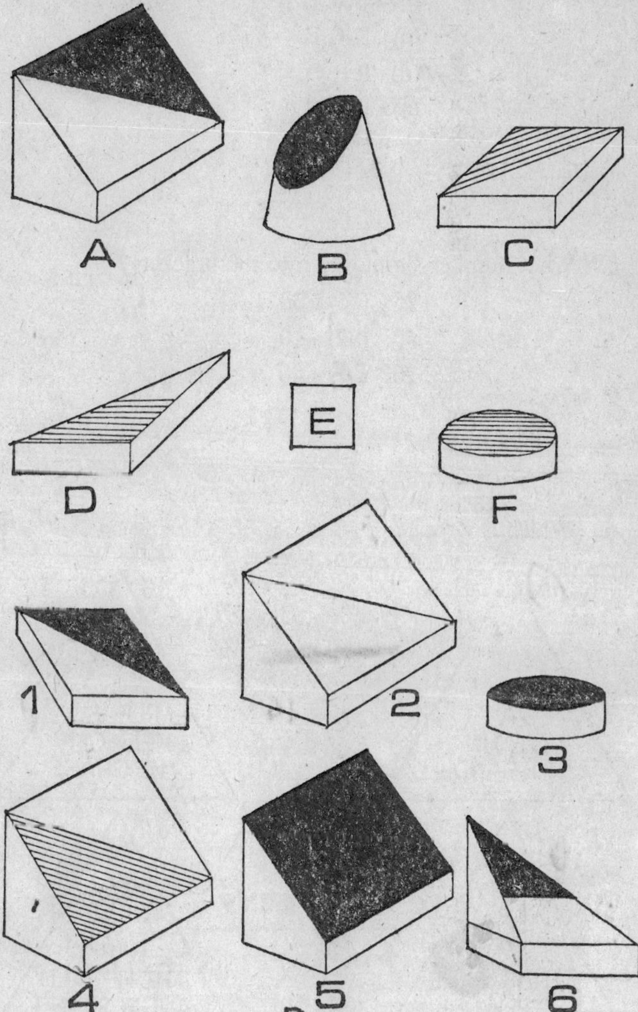

4. Which is the odd man out?

(a) M.B.E.
(b) O.B.E.
(c) K.C.B.
(d) P.R.O.
(e) D.B.E.

5. What number should go into the brackets?

25	(56)	30
45	(92)	10
20	( )	40

6. Which is wrong?

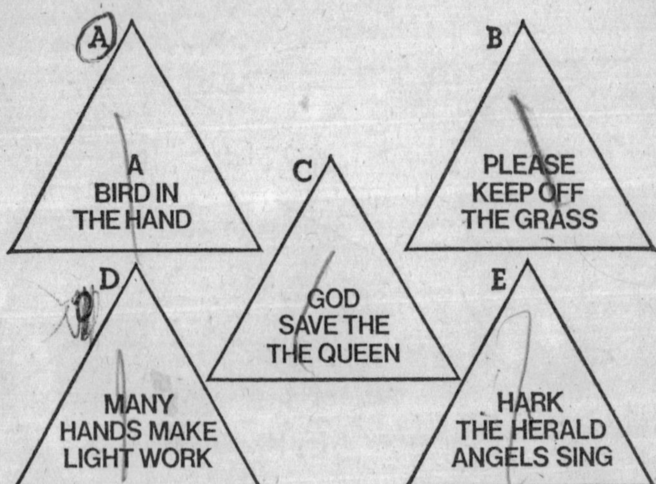

7. Which is the odd man out?

(a) MICHIGAN
(b) SUPERIOR
(c) EIRE
(d) HURON
(e) ONTARIO

8. What have these in common?

ATLANTIC
SASKATCHEWAN
SANTIAGO
SAN FRANCISCO
FRANCE

9. What words are represented by x and y?

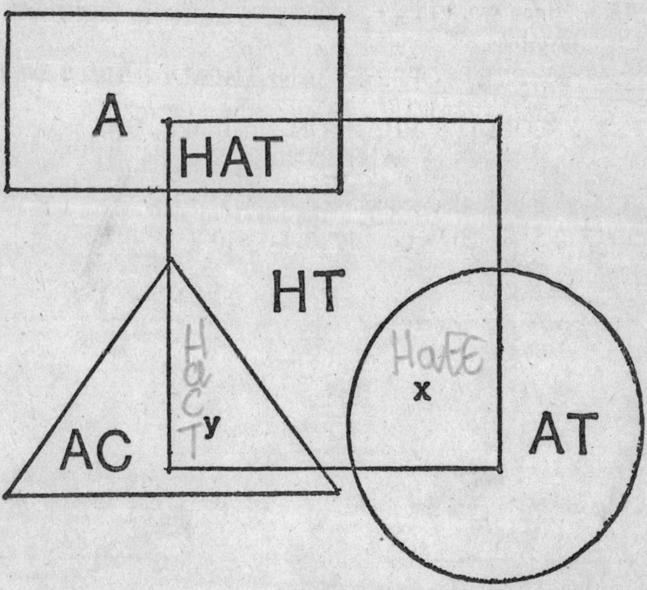

10. If TOM = 48
and DICK = 27
What is HARRY?

11. Complete this sequence:

Q P N K G —

12. Which word in the second group belongs to the first group?

EYE OPERA ANATHEMA UVULA

COLDITZ PHANTOM FYLFOT GRANGE ANTENNA EVIL

13. Complete this sequence:

20 19 17 — 10 5

14. Which one is different from the others?

A

B

C

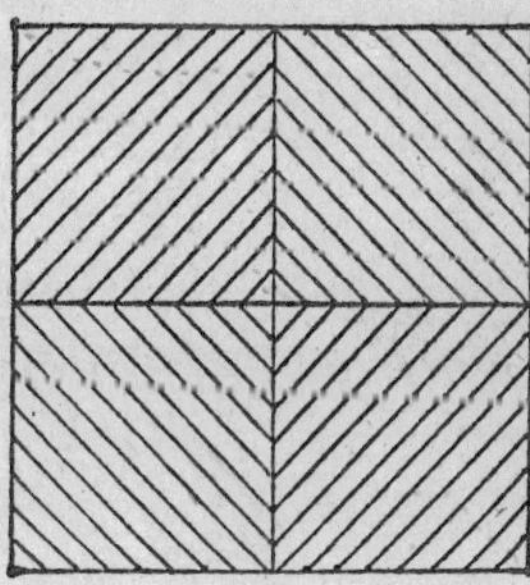

D

15. Arrange these army ranks in order of seniority, starting with the least senior.

(a) SERGEANT-MAJOR
(b) MAJOR
(c) LANCE-CORPORAL
(d) SECOND LIEUTENANT
(e) PRIVATE
(f) CAPTAIN
(g) CORPORAL
(h) LIEUTENANT
(i) SERGEANT
(j) REGIMENTAL SERGEANT-MAJOR

TEST No. 2

(Time limit: 15 minutes)

1. Which gentleman is not conforming?

2. Which is the odd man out?

(a) COSTARD

(b) NEWTON WONDER

(c) LAXTON'S FORTUNE

(d) COX'S ORANGE PIPPIN

(e) PURPLE PERSHORE

(f) BRAMLEY'S SEEDLING

3. Which cross does not conform with the others?

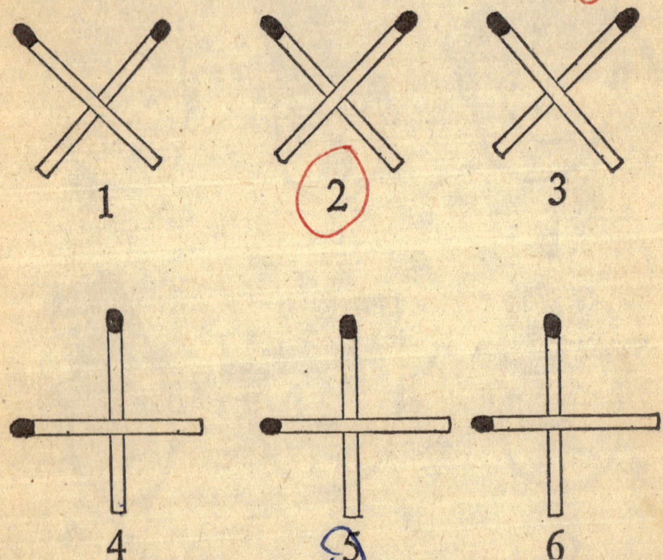

4. Which is the odd man out?

(a) POLKA
(b) MAMBA
(c) POLONAISE
(d) MAZURKA
(e) QUADRILLE
(f) LANCERS

5. Which of the numbered figures at the bottom belongs to G?

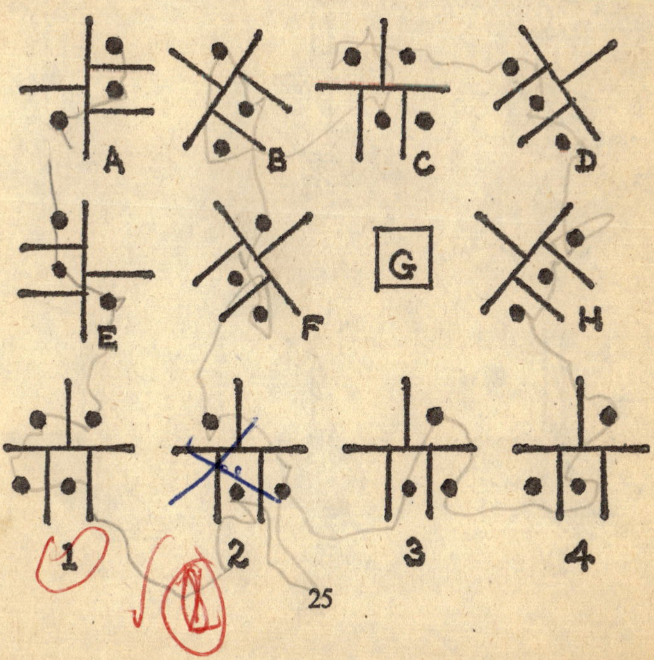

6. Which doesn't belong here?

(a) MINIM
(b) SEMIBREVE
(c) CROCHET
(d) QUAVER
(e) BREVE

7. Assuming that the top row is correct, which one is wrong in the second row?

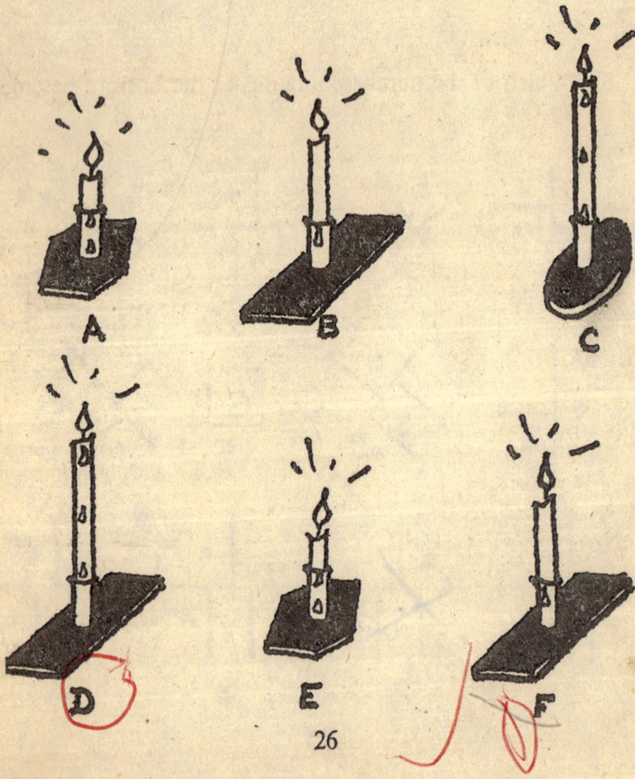

8. If DECIMAL = LADMCIE what is RECLAIM?

9. Which figure is wrong?

10. If END = FOE
what is START?

11. How many seven-lettered words can you make out of these letters?

T A R L E T S

12. *Using your eye only* (not using a pointer) and starting from the cat, which ball of string is the cat playing with?

13. Fill in the missing letters.

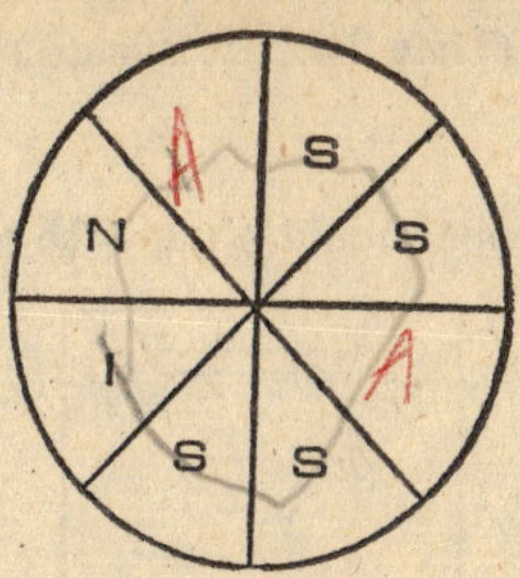

14. Here is a fruit salad. Two fruits are mixed up in each of the following, and you must use all the letters in each phrase.

1. OR I GOT REPOSE BY CAR.
2. GONE – NEAR CERTAIN.
3. ANNA AND SAMBO.

15. Which is the odd man out?

3	11	17
7	15	29

TEST No. 3

(Time limit: 20 minutes)

1. Which envelope should occupy the empty space?

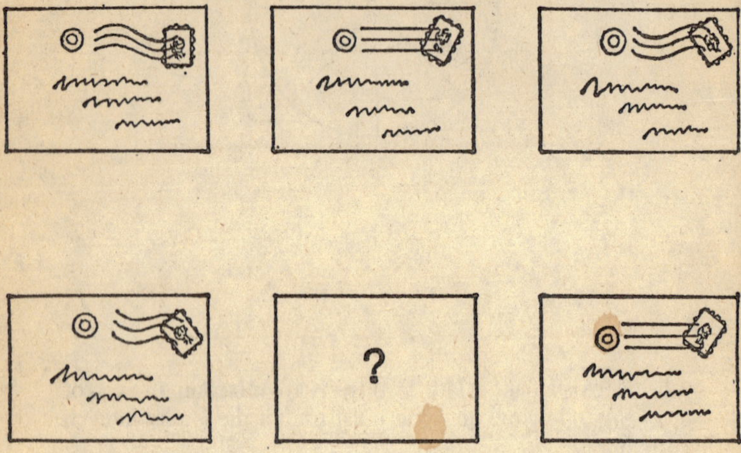

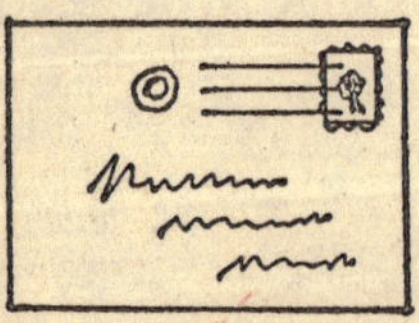

A

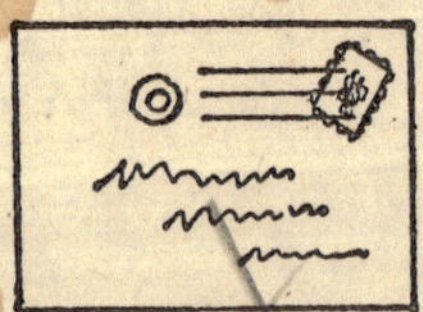

B

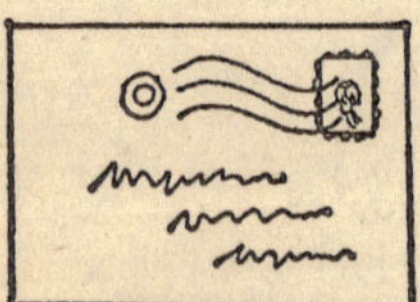

C

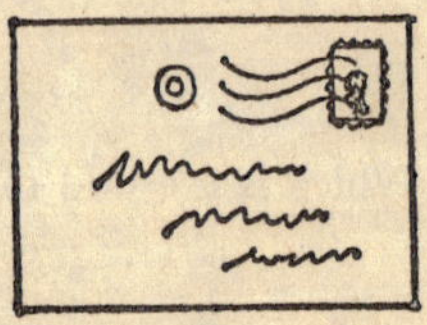

D

2. *Using your eyes only*, how many squares are there in the figure below and, assuming that A and B were joined, how many triangles?

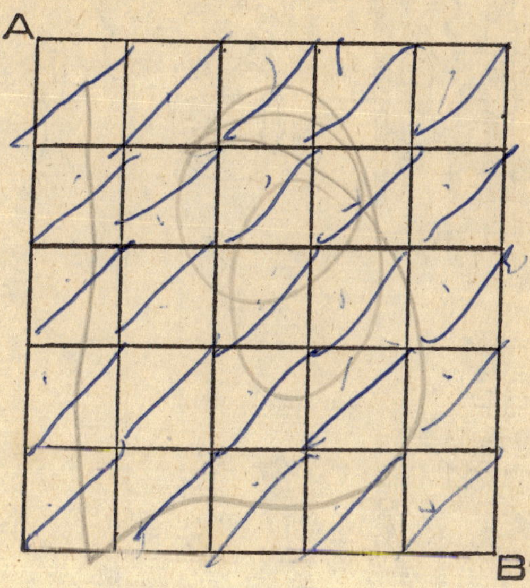

3. Which is the odd man out?

(a) Capt.

(b) L.A.C.

(c) Col.

(d) Lt.

(e) Brig.

4. Which one is out of place?

5. Which figure is wrong?

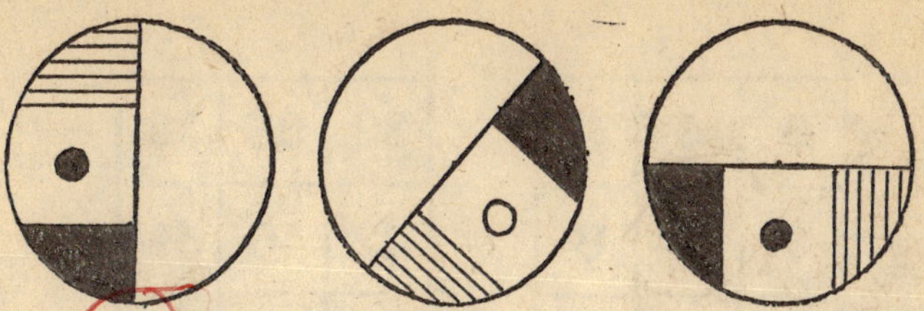

1 2 3

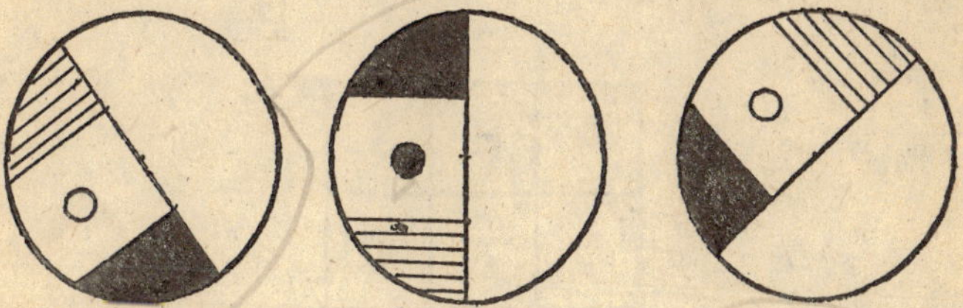

4 5 6

6. Give words to fit these definitions. *Each word must begin and end with the same two letters.*

e.g. Give back. REstoRE.

(a) TRAINED

(b) STRIP

(c) MEMBERS OF ANCIENT SECT

(d) FRUIT

(e) DEMANDING EXORBITANT INTEREST

(f) PLACE OF WORSHIP

(g) ENTHUSIASM

(h) END

(i) CRUSTACEAN

(j) VEGETABLE

7. What is the value of x in each of the following three diagrams?

5	4	9
3	5	8
2	7	x

A

32	35	39
42	46	51
3	8	x

B

A	E	J
D	x	O
F	L	S

C

8. Which is the odd man out?

(a) EVIL
(b) LIAR
(c) PERT
(d) BRAG
(e) TRAP
(f) PINS

9. What number goes into the brackets?

64	(49)	144
85	(57)	119
144	( )	90

10. What letters should fill the blank spaces?

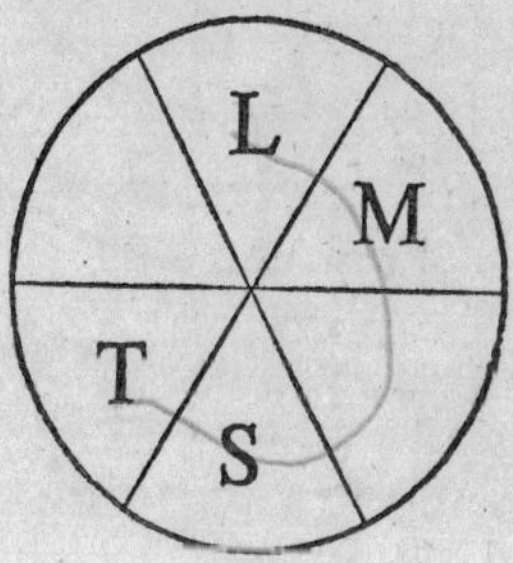

11. Which is the odd man out?

(a) CLARINET

(b) SAXOPHONE

(c) BASSOON

(d) OBOE

(e) DRUM

12. Give values for X and Y.

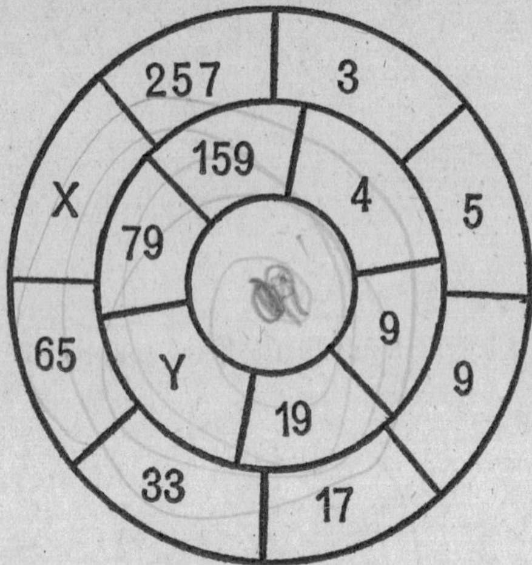

13. If GORE = ERGO
what is SPAR?

14. A heavy smoker, worried about the high cost of cigarettes, decided to economise by saving his cigarette ends and making new cigarettes from them.
He found that each cigarette end accounted for one-sixth of the whole cigarette.
He smoked 36 cigarettes a day.
By using this method, how many EXTRA cigarettes was he able to obtain in a week?

15. What three-lettered word can be added to all of the following letters to make a four-lettered word?

B
D
F
G
H
N
P
R
S
T
W

TEST No. 4

(Time limit: 15 minutes)

1. Who is the odd man out?

   (a) GERMAN
   (b) FRANCE
   (c) DVORAK
   (d) DELIBES
   (e) BERLIOZ
   (f) VERDI
   (g) SIBELIUS

2. Complete these words, for which definitions are supplied. The number of missing letters is indicated by asterisks.

1.	Resist.	**POSE
2.	Assume.	***POSE
3.	Lay on something else.	*******POSE
4.	Place upon.	**POSE
5.	Insert.	*****POSE
6.	Make up.	***POSE
7.	Propound.	***POSE
8.	Change places.	*****POSE
9.	Aim.	***POSE
10.	Unmask.	**POSE
11.	Place in order.	***POSE

3. Arrange these patterns into four pairs.

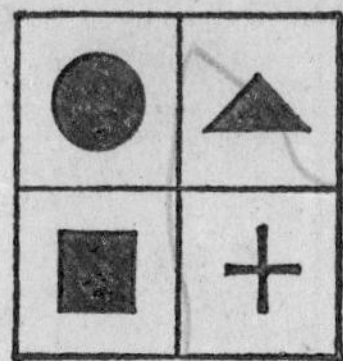

A

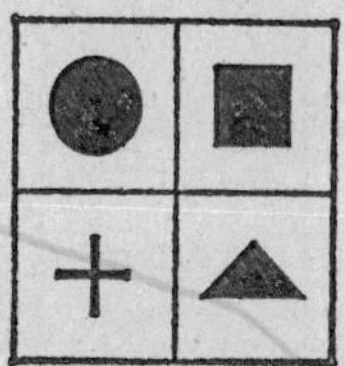

B

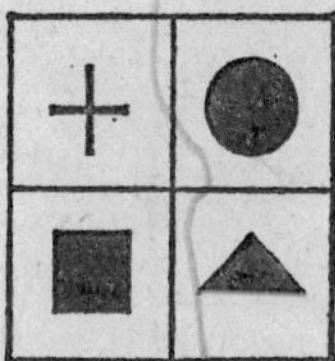

C

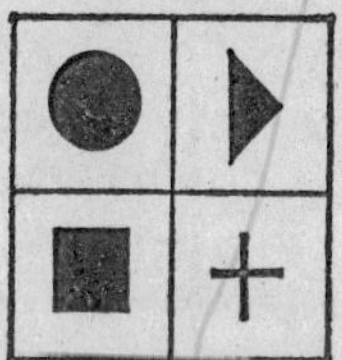

D

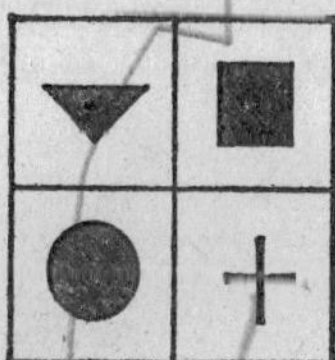

E

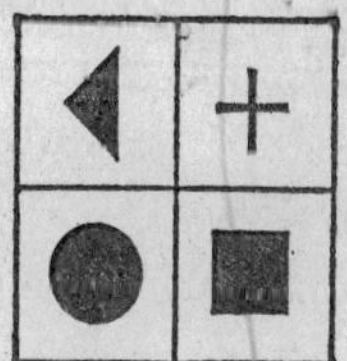

F

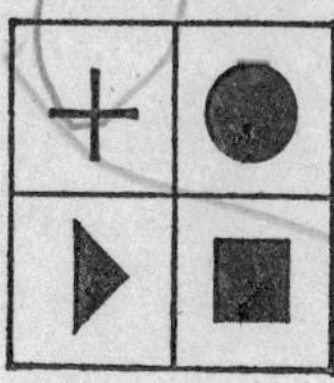

G

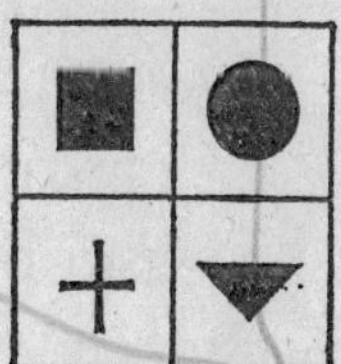

H

4. What word goes at X?

peat	sear
rase	tape

riot	gore
ogre	trio

blame	evict
X	amble

5. Which is the odd man out?

(a) CENT

(b) PESETA

(c) CENTIME

(d) ESCUDO

(e) REIS

(f) PALESTRA

6. Which bottle is wrong?

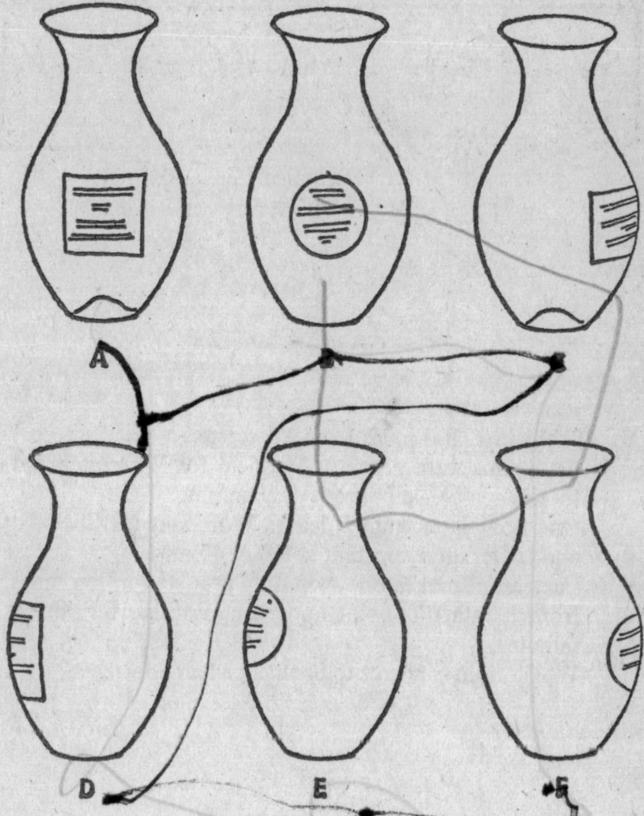

7. Changing one letter at a time, change PONY into LAMB in eight moves, using words which fit the definitions.

1.	PONY	
1.	* * * *	Small body of water
2.	* * * *	Tender and loving
3.	* * * *	Discover
4.	* * * *	Penalty
5.	* * * *	Equator
6.	* * * *	Fruit
7.	* * * *	Crippled
8.	LAMB	

8. Sheffield is 100 miles from Worcester.
At 1 p.m. train A leaves Sheffield for Worcester and travels at a constant speed of 30 m.p.h.
One hour later train B leaves Worcester for Sheffield and travels at a constant speed of 40 mp.h.
Each train makes one stop only at a station ten miles from its starting-point and remains there for fifteen minutes.
Which train is nearer to Sheffield when they meet?

9. Complete this sequence:

A C F * O U

10. Which car goes into which road?

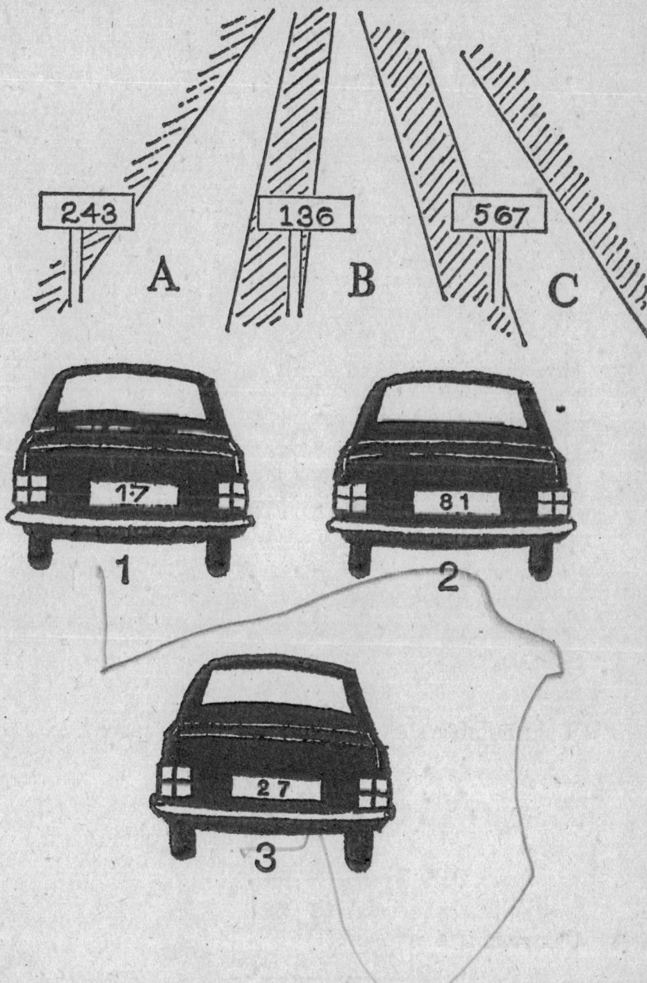

11. Which is the odd man out?

(a) STAMP

(b) STATIONARY

(c) ENVELOPE

(d) PEN

(e) POSTCARD

12. How many six-lettered words can you make from these letters?

S E N L I T

13. What number should go into the blank space?

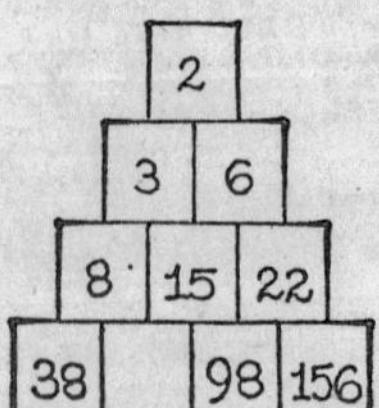

14. What word completes the first word and starts the second?

P A R A (* * *) A C E

15. Which of these patterns does not conform with the others?

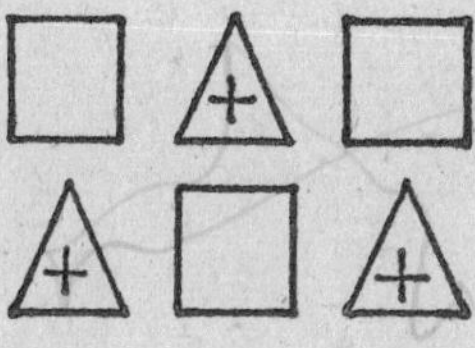

A

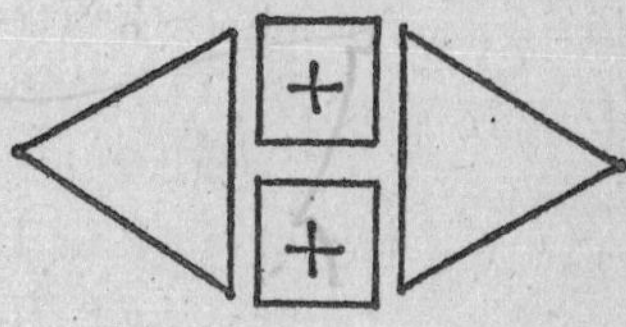

B

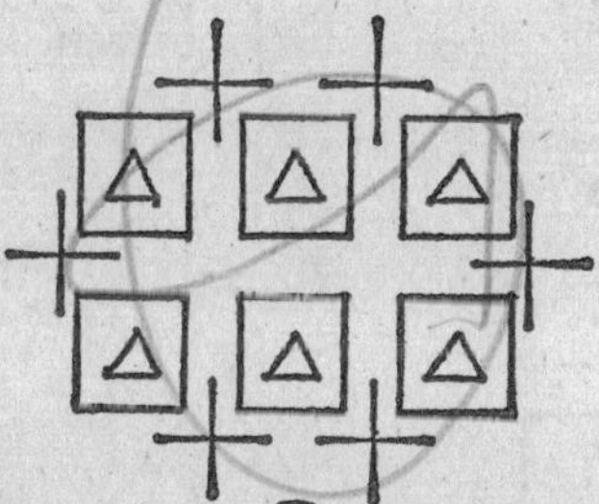

C

D

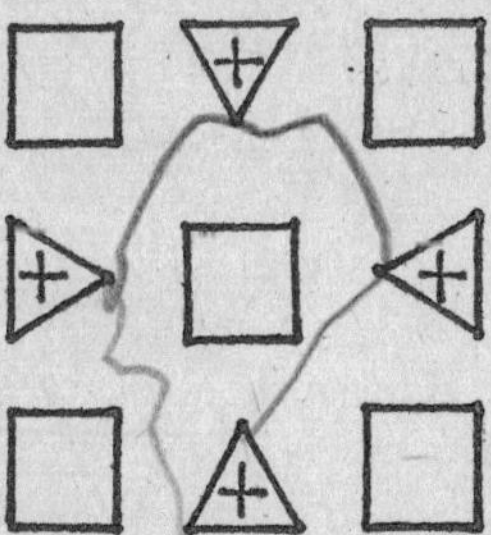

E

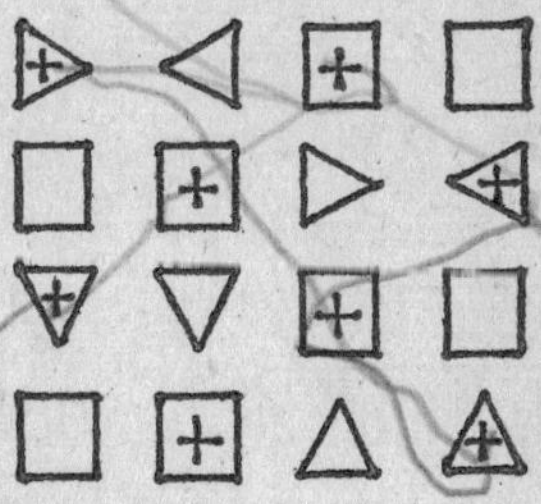

F

TEST No. 5

(Time limit: 30 minutes)

1. Which is the odd man out?

   (a) POTATO
   (b) TURNIP
   (c) PEA
   (d) PARSNIP
   (e) CARROT

2. Which of the figures at the bottom belongs to E?

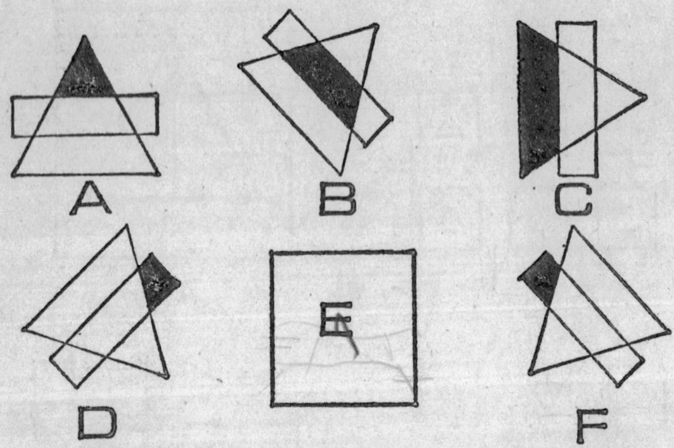

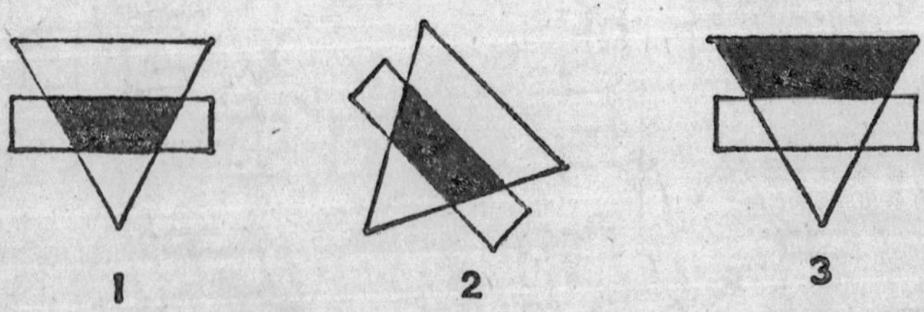

3. Which ladder is wrong?

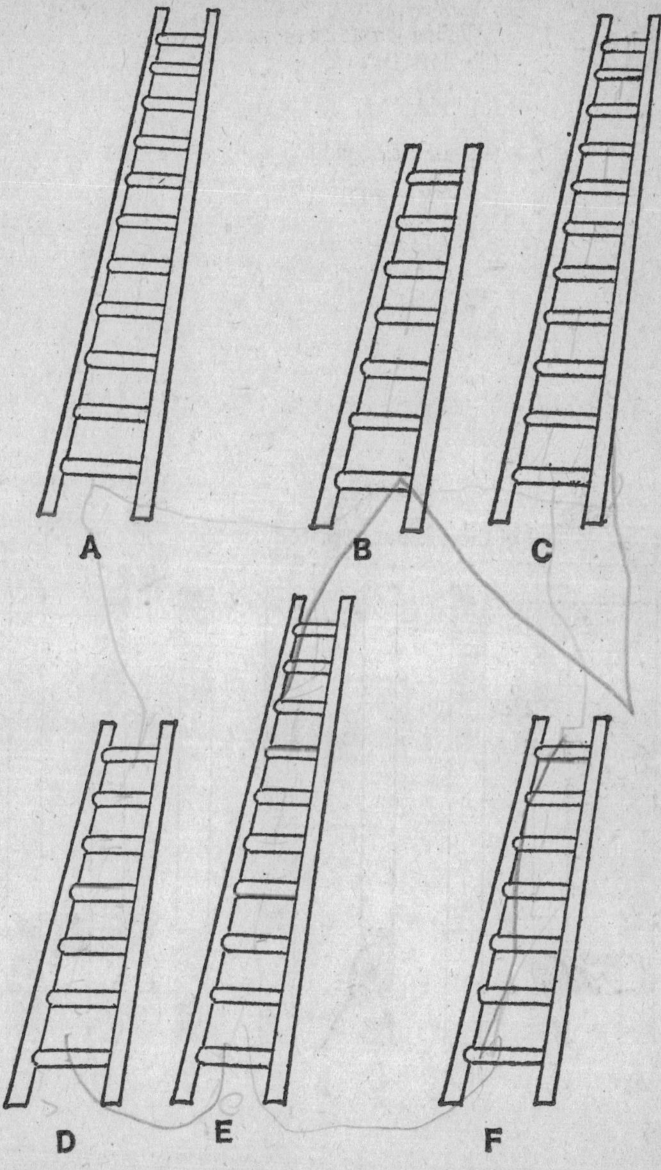

4. Which is the odd man out?

(a) CIVIC

(b) DRUID

(c) KAYAK

(d) LEVEL

(e) FRETFUL

(f) ELOPE

5. Which of these is out of place?

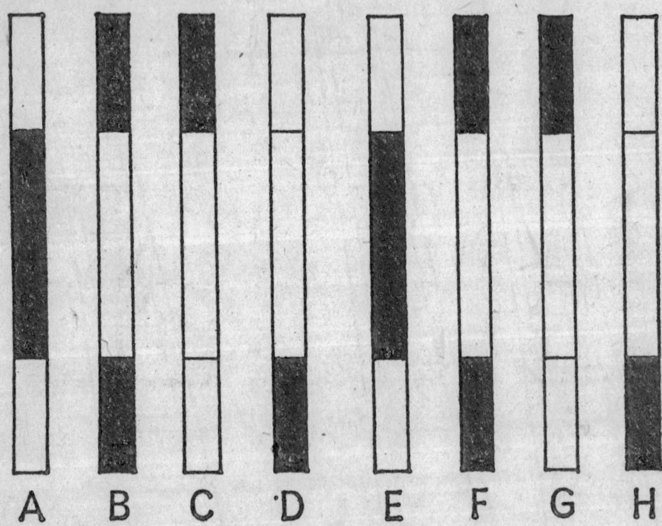

6. Arrange these patterns into four pairs.

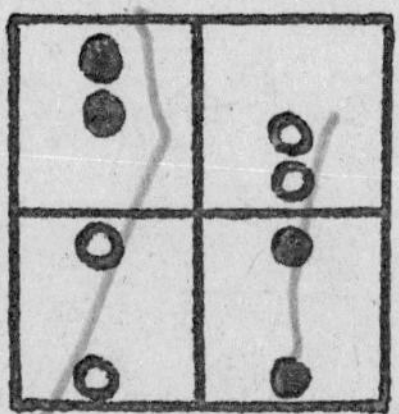
A

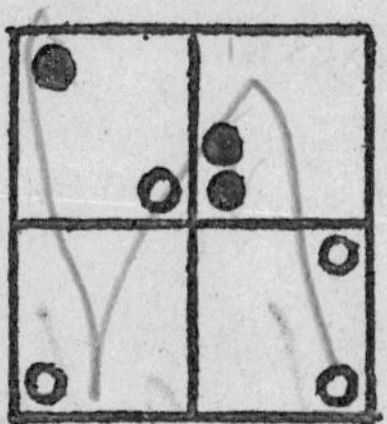
B

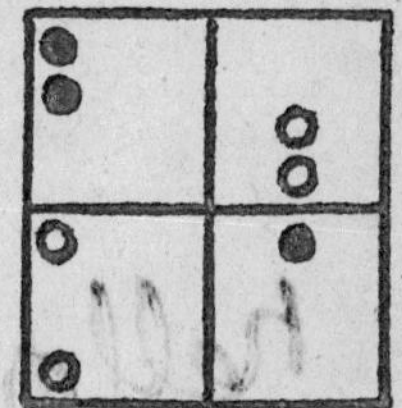
C

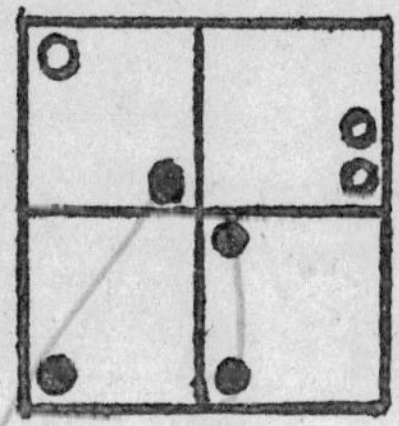
D

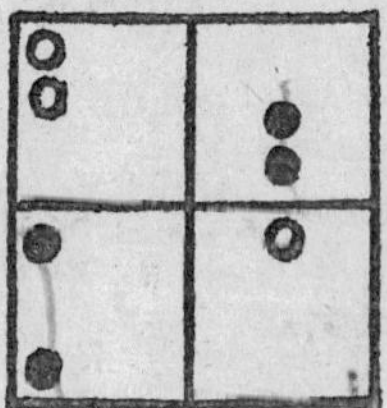
E

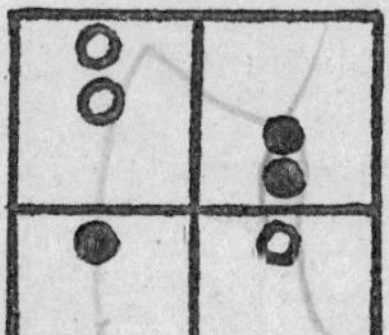
F

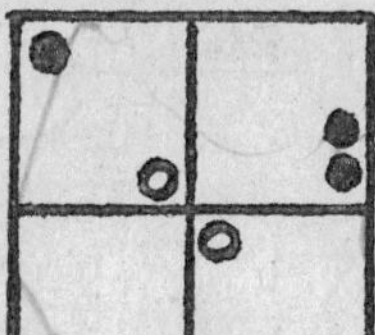
G

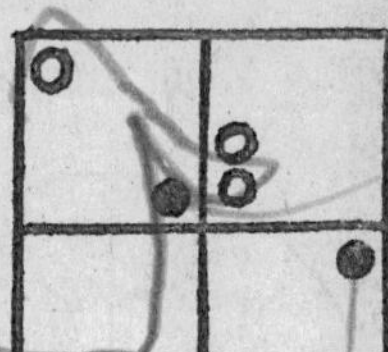
H

7. What numbers belong to a and b?

36 (35) 60

65 (58) 104

a (79) b

8. What have these three words in common?

ALMOST

ADEPT

DEFY

9. What numbers should take the place of A and B?

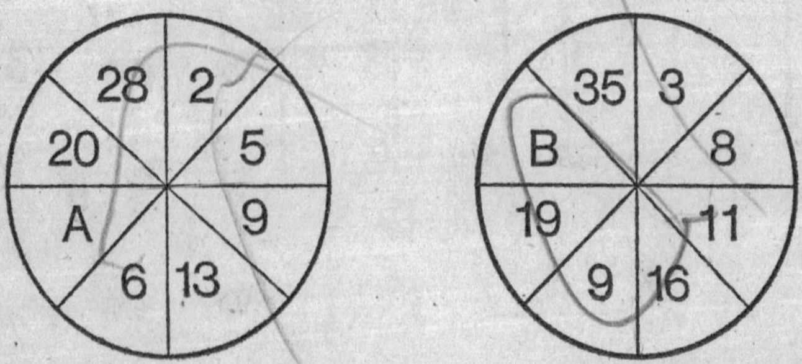

10. Which of the letters at the bottom should take the place of X?

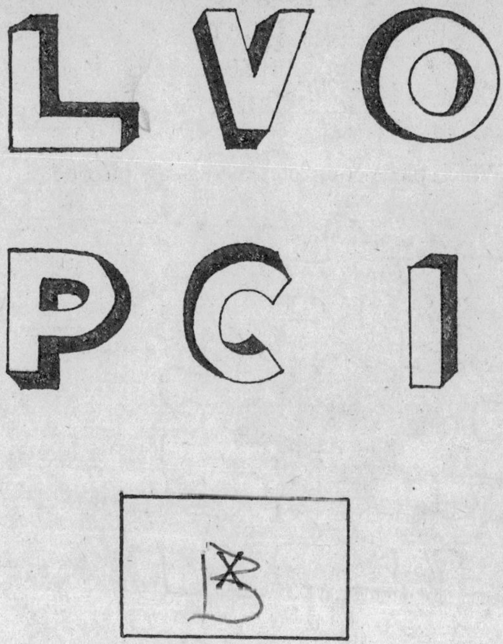

A

B

C

D

11. Which is the odd man out?

(a) ECLAP
(b) YSORT
(c) PHYPA
(d) QREAT

12. Which piece completes the jig-saw puzzle?

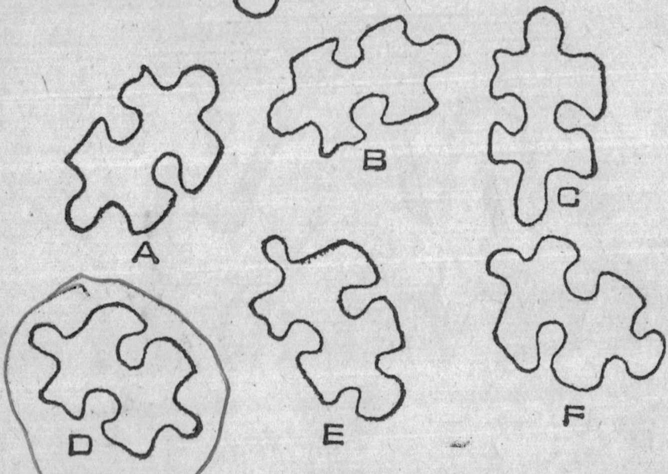

13. *Using your eye only* (not using a pointer), which footballer has scored the goal? (You must not start from the goalkeeper.)

14. Murmansk, in Russia, is on longitude 33 degrees east. Victoria Island, off Canada, is on longitude 110 degrees west.
If you travelled due east from the North Pole, which would you reach first?

15. Assuming that houses A, B, C and D are correct which of the numbered houses at the bottom are incorrect?

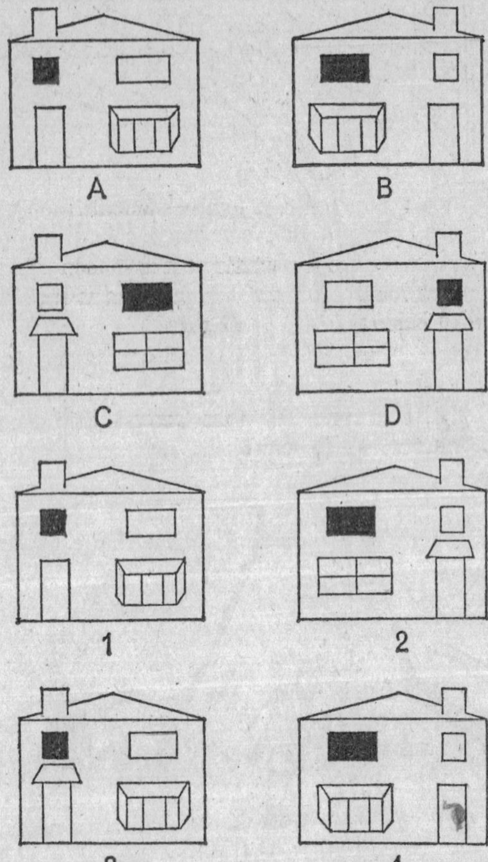

ANSWERS

TEST No. 1

1. (c) PEACOCK, which is masculine. All the others are feminine. **(1 point)**

2. F. The light ale should be in the tumblers and the dark ale in the tankards. **(1 point)**

3. 6. Shapes with inclined top faces are heavily shaded; shapes with flat tops are lightly shaded. If the top face is straight-edged only half of it is shaded; if the top face has a round edge the whole of it is shaded. Therefore, 6, which has an inclined top face and is half-heavily-shaded belongs to E. **(2 points)**

4. (d) P.R.O. (Public Relations Officer). The others are decorations. **(1 point)**

5. 48. The numbers outside the brackets are divided by 5 and the results placed inside the brackets. **(1 point)**

6. C. Look carefully and you will see that it reads: 'God Save THE THE Queen.' Not a catch, since the words were plainly to be seen, but if you fell for it it proves that the eye sees what it *wants* to see, and not what it really sees. **(1 point)**

7. (c) EIRE. The Great Lakes of Canada are assembled

here, except for this name for Ireland. (The name of the Lake is, of course, ERIE). **(1 point)**

8. They all contain the letters AN. **(1 point)**

9. x=THAT

   y=CHAT

   The overlapping shapes combine the letters contained in the individual shapes (A for a rectangle; HT for a square; AC for a triangle, and AT for a circle). These are the only words that can be formed from the combined letters, just as, in the example shown, HAT is the only word that can be formed from a combination of A and HT. **(1 point for each. Maximum 2 points)**

10. 70. Find the number in the alphabet of each letter and add them together.

    T=20; O=15; M=13. 20+15+13=48

    D=4; I=9; C=3; K=11. 4+9+3+11=27

    H=8; A=1; R=18; R=18; Y=25. 8+1+18+18+25=70 **(1 point)**

11. B. The sequence descends alphabetically, first to the next letter, then skipping one, then two, and so forth. **(1 point)**

12. ANTENNA. All the words in the first group start and end with a vowel. ANTENNA is the only word in the second group that does so. **(1 point)**

13. 14. The series is a reducing one, reducing by 1, 2, 3, 4 and 5. Therefore 17 reduces by 3 to become 14. **(1 point)**

14. C. In the top right-hand quarter there are only 14 hatch-lines, whereas in all the other quarters there are 15. **(1 point)**

15. e c g i a j d h f b
PRIVATE
LANCE-CORPORAL
CORPORAL
SERGEANT
SERGEANT-MAJOR
REGIMENTAL SERGEANT-MAJOR
SECOND LIEUTENANT
LIEUTENANT
CAPTAIN
MAJOR
(1 point)

TEST No. 2

1. I – has had a shave! **(1 point)**

2. (e) PURPLE PERSHORE – the only plum among the apples. **(1 point)**

3. 2. When the head of the match points to the left, that match should lie on top of the other match. In 2 it lies underneath. **(1 point)**

4. (b) MAMBA, which is a snake. The others are dances. **(1 point)**

5. 1. In the top row the figure is rotated $\frac{1}{4}$ turn clockwise and the position of the dots changes. In the second row the figure is rotated $\frac{1}{4}$ turn anti-clockwise and the position of the dots changes as in the first row. **(2 points)**

6. (c) CROCHET (needlework). Not to be confused with CROTCHET, which, like the others, is a musical note. **(1 point)**

7. D. This candlestick should have an oval base. **(1 point)**

8. MIRACLE. The letters of the first word have been re-arranged in the order: 7, 6, 1, 5, 3, 4, 2, so the letters in RECLAIM must be re-arranged in the same order. **(1 point)**

9. 7. The triangles should overlap. In each row across there is a large and a small shape, with one figure encircling the other (1, 6 and 8); one outside the other (2, 4 and 9); and both figures overlapping (3, 5 and 7 – which SHOULD do so, but doesn't). **(2 points)**

10. TUBSU. Each letter of the first word is advanced one position in the alphabet to form the second word. **(2 points)**

11. Five: STARLET, TELSTAR, STARTLE, RATTLES. **(1 point for each word. Maximum: 4 points)**

12. B. **(1 point)**

13. A in each case, the word being ASSASSIN.
(1 point, but only if both correct)

14. 1. GOOSEBERRY, APRICOT
2. ORANGE, NECTARINE
3. BANANA, DAMSON
(1 point for each word. Maximum: 6 points)

15. 15. All the others are prime numbers. **(2 points)**

TEST No. 3

1. C. Each row contains one envelope with an upright stamp, one with the stamp sloping to the right and one to the left. The upright stamp (the missing one in the second row) should be cancelled with wavy lines to correspond with the first envelope in the top row, and C is the only one which so conforms. **(1 point)**

2. 55 squares and 30 triangles.
(1 point for each. Maximum: 2 points)

3. (b) L.A.C. (Leading Aircraftman.) This is the only R.A.F. rank, the others being army ranks. **(1 point)**

4. The football. There are four golf accessories, four chess accessories and four snooker accessories. **(1 point)**

5. 1. From 2 onwards the figure is rotated clockwise, 45 degrees at a time. In each movement the spot alternates from white to black, the heavy and light-shaded portions being alternately transposed in their positions. No. 1 should be as follows:

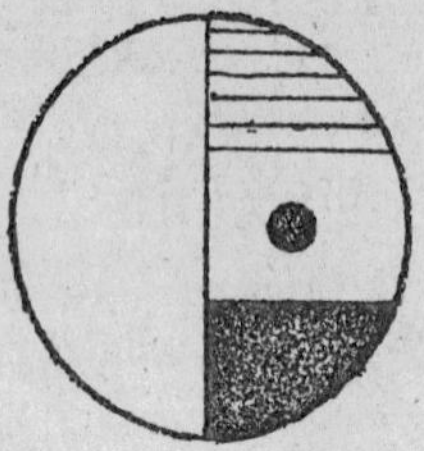

(2 points)

6. (a) EDUCATED
   (b) DENUDE
   (c) ESSENES
   (d) NECTARINE
   (e) USURIOUS
   (f) CHURCH
   (g) VERVE
   (h) TERMINATE
   (i) SHELLFISH
   (j) ONION

   (Score 1 point for 6 or more correct, 2 points if all correct. Maximum: 2 points)

7. A x=9. The figure in the third square across is the sum of the figures in the preceding two squares.

   B x=14. In the first row across the numbers increase by 3 and 4; in the second row by 4 and 5. Therefore, in the third row they should increase by 5 and 6.

C x=I. This is similar to the previous example, except that letters are used instead of numbers. In the first row the letters advance, skipping 3 and 4 places respectively. In the second row they should advance, skipping 4 and 5 places, so as to conform with the third row, in which the letters skip 5 and 6 places.

(1 point for each correct answer. Maximum: 3 points)

8. PERT. All the other words form another word when they are spelt backwards – LIVE, RAIL, GARB, PART, SNIP. **(2 points)**

9. 85. In the first row the numbers outside the brackets are divided by 16 and the results placed inside the brackets. In the second row they are divided by 17. Therefore, in the third row they are divided by 18. **(2 points)**

10. A and O, to make the word 'ALMOST'. **(1 point, but only if both correct)**

11. (e) DRUM (a percussion instrument). All the others are wind instruments. **(1 point)**

12. X=129. In the outer ring, moving clockwise, each number is doubled and 1 subtracted from the result.

Y=39. In the inner ring, moving clockwise, each number is doubled and 1 added to the result.

(1 point for each correct answer. Maximum: 2 points)

13. RASP. The order of the letters in each case is changed from 1, 2, 3, 4 to 4, 3, 1, 2. **(1 point)**

14. 8 and 1/6th cigarettes.
(Score 2 points for correct answer and 1 point if you have answered 8 cigarettes)

15. EAR. (The words become: bear, dear, fear, gear, hear, near, pear, rear, sear, tear and wear.) **(1 point)**

TEST No. 4

1. (b) FRANCE (Anatole), who was a writer. The others were composers. **(1 point)**

1. OPPOSE
2. SUPPOSE
3. SUPERIMPOSE
4. IMPOSE
5. INTERPOSE
6. COMPOSE
7. PROPOSE
8. TRANSPOSE
9. PURPOSE
10. EXPOSE
11. DISPOSE

(Score 1 point for each word. Maximum: 11 points)

3. AF, BG, CE, DH.
(1 point – but only if all correct)

4. CIVET. In each square the opposite words are anagrams of each other. The only possible anagram of EVICT is CIVET. **(1 point)**

5. (f) PALESTRA, which is a gymnasium. The others are units of currency. **(2 points)**

6. D, which should have a false bottom. Bottles with round labels have flat bases and bottles with square labels have false bottoms. **(1 point)**

7. PONY
   1. POND
   2. FOND
   3. FIND
   4. FINE
   5. LINE
   6. LIME
   7. LAME
   8. LAMB

   (Score 1 point for 5 words correct or 2 points for 7)

8. They are both the same distance from Sheffield *when they meet*! (Another example of reading the question carefully before giving an answer.) **(1 point)**

9. J. The letters advance alphabetically, first skipping one, then two letters, and so forth. After F, skip three letters to reach J. **(1 point)**

10. Car 1 goes into road B, because 17 goes into 136;

Car 2 goes into road C, because 81 goes into 567;
Car 3 goes into road A, because 27 goes into 243.
(Score 1 point for each. Maximum: 3 points)

11. (b) STATIONARY, which means: 'not moving.' The other words apply to correspondence (as also would 'stationery'). **(1 point)**

12. *FIVE.* TINSEL, SILENT, ENLIST, LISTEN, INLETS.
(Score 1 point for each. Maximum: 5 points)

13. 59. Proceeding from top to bottom, along the rows from left to right, add the two previous numbers and add 1, then add the two previous numbers and subtract 1, and so forth, adding 1 and subtracting 1 alternately. Thus the two numbers previous to the blank square are 22 and 38. These are added together, giving 60, and 1 subtracted from the total. **(2 points)**

14. SOL. (PARASOL and SOLACE.) **(1 point)**

15. E. All of the figures except E consist of an equal number of squares, triangles and crosses. In E there are four triangles and crosses but five squares. **(2 points)**

TEST No. 5

1. (c) PEA. The other vegetables are root crops. **(1 point)**

2. 1. The figure is turned 45 degrees clockwise each time. the black shaded portion moves first from top to bottom (in the first row) and then from left to right (in the second row). **(2 points)**

3. E, which has an even number of rungs. All the others have an odd number. **(1 point)**

4. (e) FRETFUL. All the others begin and end with the same letter. **(2 points)**

5. E, which should be moved slightly to the left, so that they are all equidistant. (The design is quite in order, but probably diverted your attention from the spacing.) **(1 point)**

6. AF, BH, CE, DG. **(1 point)**

7. a=98

   b=126

   In the first row the numbers outside the brackets are divided by 12 and the results placed inside the brackets; in the second row they are divided by 13; thus, in the third row the numbers inside the brackets are multiplied by 14 to obtain a and b. **(2 points)**

8. The letters of each word are in alphabetic order. **(2 points)**

9. A: 12 (Each number doubles its opposite lower
5 number and adds two.)

B: 25 (Each number doubles its opposite lower number and adds three.)

(Score 1 point for each: Maximum 2 points)

10. B. The 'block' of the letter (the shaded part which seems to make the letter stand out) is placed in the following way:

(a) On the right and above if the letter consists only of straight strokes, either vertical or horizontal.

(b) On the right and below if the letter consists of straight *and* curved strokes.

(c) On the left and below if the letter consists of straight strokes which are *not* vertical or horizontal.

(d) On the left and above if the letter is entirely curved.

(3 points)

11. (d) QREAT. All the others are anagrams of words: ECLAP=PLACE, YSORT=STORY; PHYPA=HAPPY.

(2 points)

12. A. **(1 point)**

13. B has scored the goal. **(1 point)**

14. You can only travel south from the North Pole! **(1 point)**

15. Examination of the four correct houses gives the following information:

(a) The front door is on the same side as the chimney.
(b) If the front door is on the left, the lower window is a bay window *if there is no porch over the door.*
(c) Also, if the front door is on the left, there is a black window over the door if there is no porch and a white window if there *is* a porch.
(d) If the front door is on the right, again there is a bay window if there is no porch over the door and a rectangular window if there is.
(e) If the front door is on the right, however, the window over the door is reversed from previously, that is, if there is no porch there is a white window over the door and if there *is* a porch there is a black window.

Comparing the four numbered houses with this information we find:

(i) House No. 1 is correct (front door on left, black window over door and lower bay-window).
(ii) House No. 2 is incorrect because the window over the porch should be black and that over the lower window should be white.
(iii) House No. 3 is incorrect because not only is there a bay window in addition to a porch, but the upper windows are also wrong.
(iv) House No. 4 is correct and conforms with House B.

Therefore, 2 and 3 are incorrect.
(1 point for each right answer. Maximum: 2 points)

GROUP I

Ratings for Tests 1–5

The total score possible for these five tests is 127 points, made up as follows:

TEST No. 1	17 points
TEST No. 2	27 points
TEST No. 3	24 points
TEST No. 4	35 points
TEST No. 5	24 points

Points are only scored for answers given within the specified time limits.

A score of 100 or over is very good indeed, and you should be able to tackle the next group of more difficult tests with greater confidence.

Between 85 and 100 points is about 'average', so there is no need to feel that there is anything wrong with your intelligence.

Between 50 and 85 points implies that perhaps you have not yet acquired the knack of working out these types of problems. Maybe you could improve your vocabulary or numerical ability, though your reasoning and visual perception are probably satisfactory. If you go through them all again, now that you are at liberty to look up the answers at the same time, you will understand the underlying ideas behind them and be able to continue with the next group with greater success.

Under 50 points! Well, what can I say? Never mind! Carry on with the next group. I have a strong feeling your ratings will not improve with the more difficult problems to come, but you will gain some experience of these sort of tests, which may stand you in good stead if you have to undergo one at any time in the future.

GROUP II

TESTS 6–10

Fairly Difficult

Vocabulary	34%
Reasoning and deduction	25%
Numerical	14%
Knowledge	16%
Visuo-spatial	7%
Visual perception	4%

TEST No. 6

(Time limit: 45 minutes)

1. Find words that will fit the definitions below. Each word must contain the name of an animal (e.g. 'Writing material' – p APE r). The number of letters in each word is shown in brackets.

(a) Patience (11)
(b) Colouring matter (7)
(c) Injure (6)
(d) Musical instrument (7)
(e) Lucky charm (6)
(f) Horse (8)
(g) Laying down the law (8)
(h) Become motionless (8)
(i) Seize for military service (10)
(j) Exuberant (9)

2. Give values for X and Y in the third square.

6	7
42	1764

8	3
24	576

3	2
X	Y

3. Which is the odd man out?

(a) Quite an excellent zoo can be seen at Keswick. Jaguars, vixen, hyenas and mice from Peru are there.

(b) The lazy people like resting quite often, but excessively wakeful men just don't.

(c) The quick brown fox jumped over the lazy dog.

4. What should go into the last circle?

5. Which of the numbered triangles belongs to x?

6. What countries are these?

(a) B V T U S B M J B

(b) K P F K C

(c) F Q D D B D

7. Start with DOZEN and end with TWENTY. Each word begins with the last two letters of the previous word *reversed.*

The clues are not in the right order, but the number of letters in each word is shown in brackets.

DOZEN

French city (5)

Amphibian that went wrong! (4)

He doesn't usually live far away (9)

Liquid measure (5)

Truly pastoral! (5)

The language of ancient Rome (5)

Mistake (5)

It means nothing to a footballer (3)

TWENTY

8. (i) Which globe in the second line should be placed at X?

(ii) Which globe in the bottom line should be placed at Y?

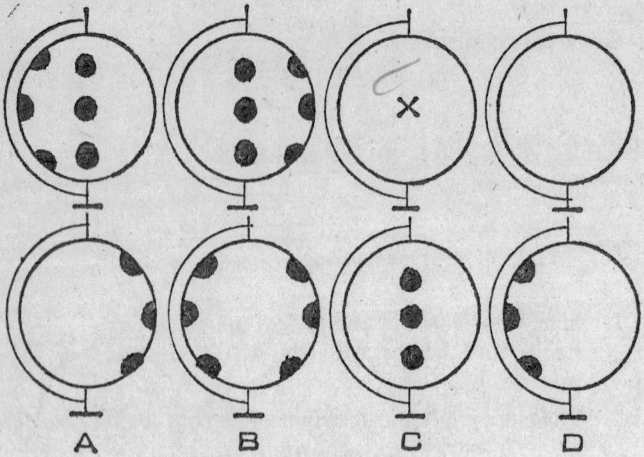

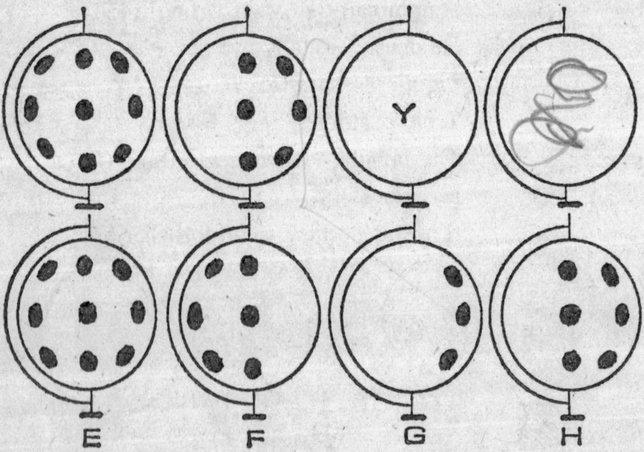

9. Which is the odd man out?

(a) HABAKKUK
(b) PHILEMON
(c) NEHEMIAH
(d) OBADIAH
(e) ZECHARIAH

10. Complete this sequence:

7 91 11 143 16 208 — —

11. Which figure is wrong?

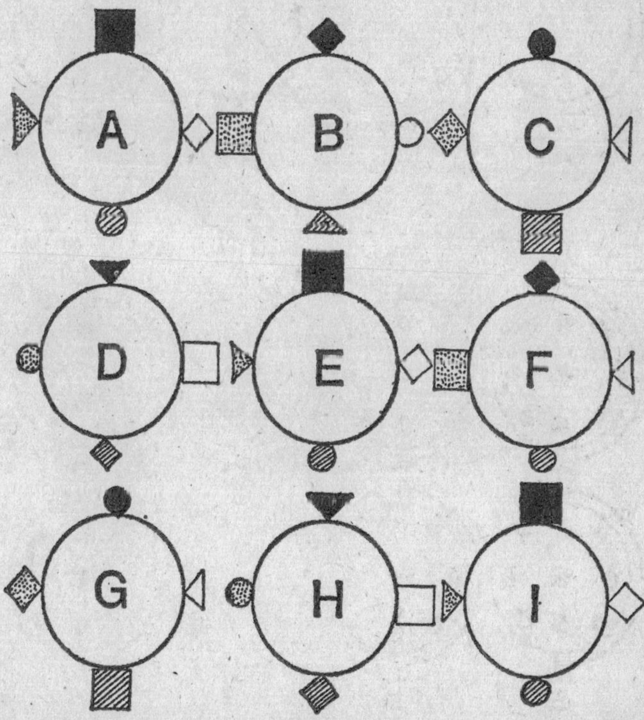

12. Which shape will complete the hexagon?

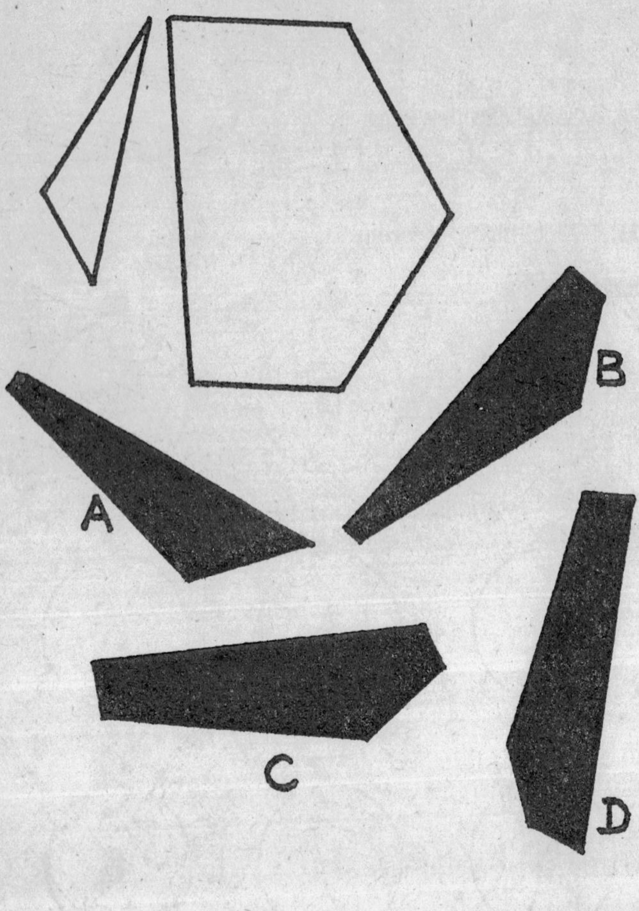

13. Which of these musical instruments are wrong?

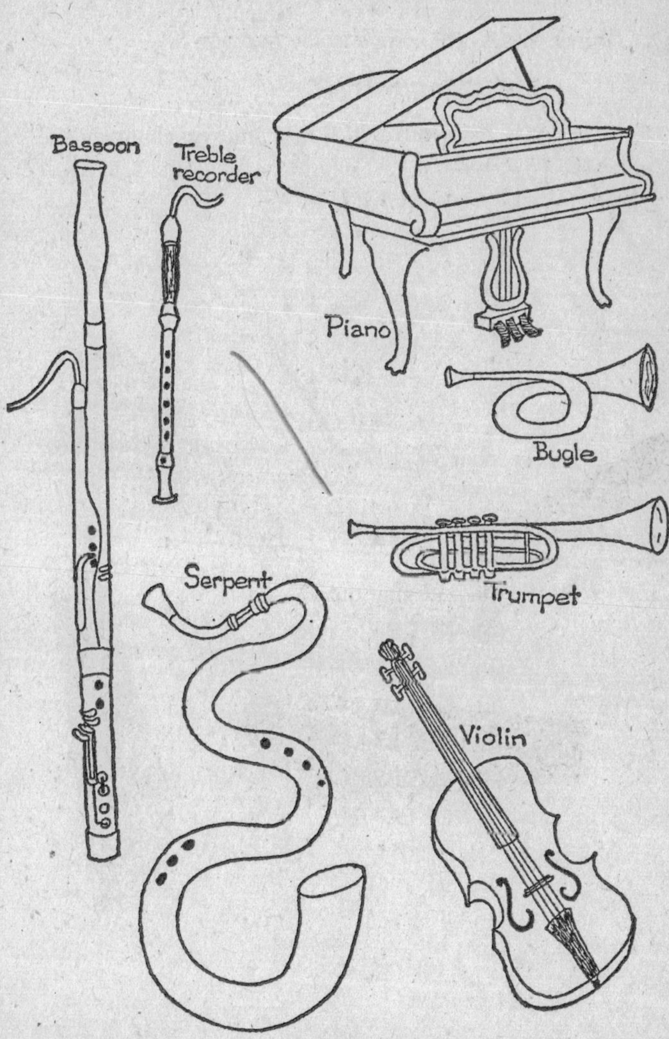

14. Change PUMA into VOLE in six moves, changing one letter at a time.

	P U M A
1.	* * * *
2.	* * * *
3.	* * * *
4.	* * * *
5.	* * * *
6.	V O L E

15. Which is the odd man out?

(a) KERRY
(b) KENTUCKY
(c) UTAH
(d) ALABAMA
(e) MISSISSIPPI
(f) OREGON

TEST No. 7

(Time limit: 40 minutes)

1. Can you compose music? Study the music below and decide which of the numbered symbols belong to (A) and (B).

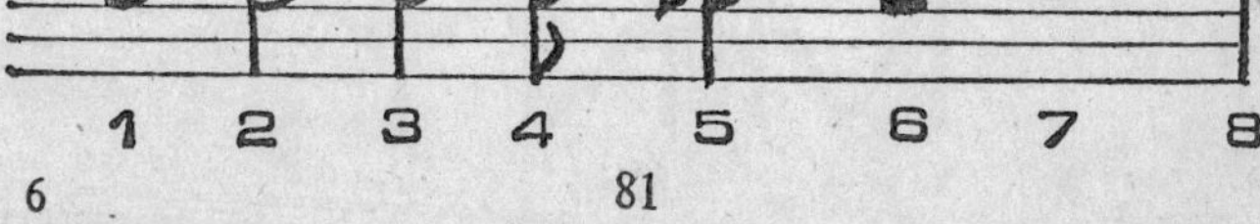

2. What numbers are represented by A and B?

4	5	6
7	8	1
5	3	A
B	9	7
9	9	1
7	6	7

3. Which letter does not belong here?

WAX

EHT

MNY

4. Which is the odd man out?

(a) CLOVE HITCH
(b) GRANNY
(c) SHEEPSHANK
(d) REEF
(e) CAT'S CRADLE

5. Which of the numbered figures at the bottom belongs to X?

6. If this design were turned 90 degrees clockwise and then held in front of a mirror, which of the designs below would be reflected?

A

B

C

D

7. Find words to suit these definitions. Every word must contain the word 'PART'.

(a) DEFENCE
(b) EAT
(c) WITTY RETORT
(d) ROOM
(e) BIRD
(f) BIASED
(g) PORTION
(h) ASSOCIATE
(i) FRENCH DISTRICT
(j) COMMUNICATE

8. Which is the odd word out?

(a) INDIA
(b) ICELAND
(c) AFRICA
(e) GREENLAND
(f) EIRE
(g) PORTUGAL
(h) FRANCE

9. Complete this sequence:

2 3 4 9 16 81 256 *

10. Which piece will complete No. 1?

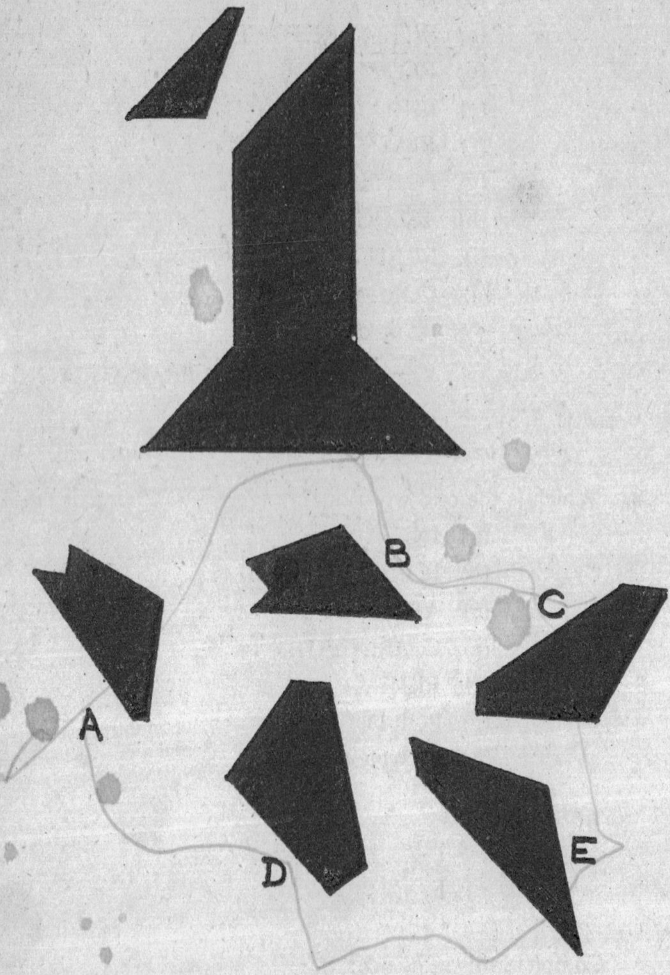

11. Which one is different?

(a) EROICA
(b) PASTORALE
(c) CHORAL
(d) EMPEROR
(e) TOY

12. Find words which satisfy EACH definition:

ARREST – UNDERSTAND
EXCAVATION – POSSESSIVE PRONOUN
CLIMB – PART OF FISH
SHOE – RAISE WATER
BADGER'S BURROW – GROUP OF GAMES
CHARACTER – MISSIVE
WORKERS – STICK
GAS-JET – ROAD

13. Which is the odd man out?

(a) BECOMES
(b) FACETIOUS
(c) CEMENT
(d) ACCORDING
(e) ABSTEMIOUS

14. How many revolutions of A will take place in order to bring the black teeth into mesh with each other:

(a) If A rotates clockwise;

(b) If A rotates anti-clockwise?

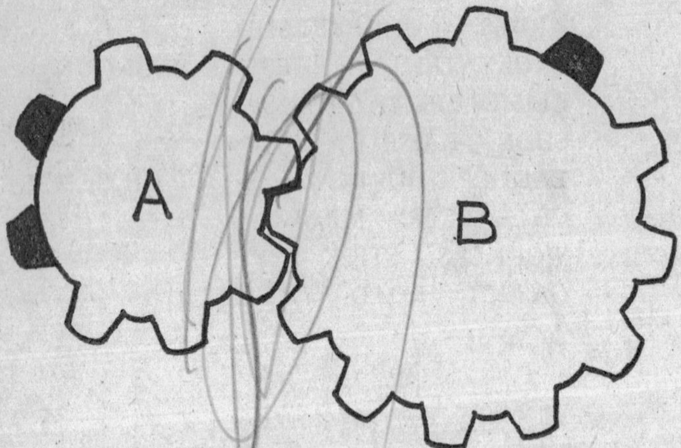

15. Which signal is wrong? (The arrow indicates the direction of operation of the signal.)

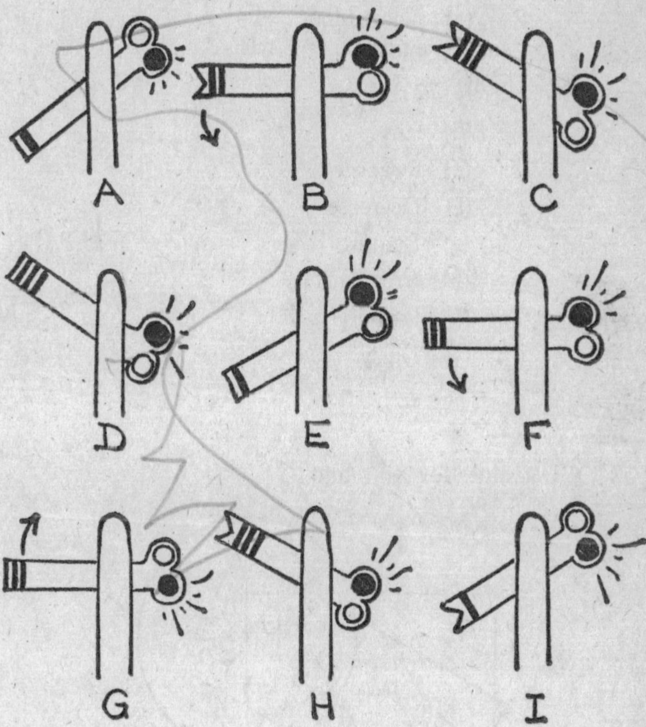

TEST No. 8

(Time limit: 45 minutes)

1. Find the words for which definitions are given. Each word must contain the word: WAN.

(a) Nasal tone
(b) Baton
(c) Tree
(d) Rove
(e) Swagger
(f) Decrease
(g) Require
(h) Irresponsible
(i) Bird
(j) Daisy

2. Give values for X, Y and Z.

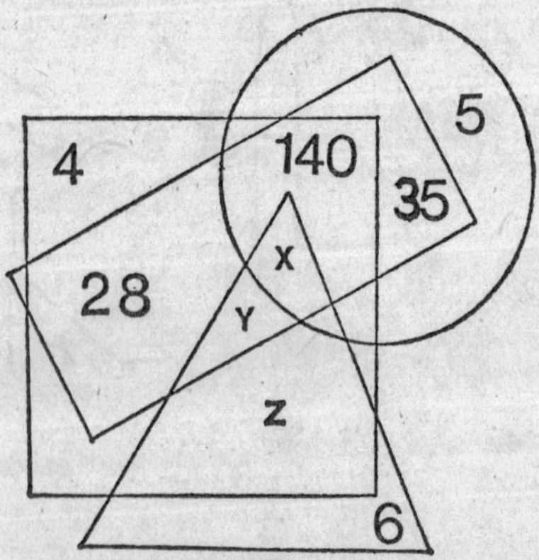

3. Which is the odd man out?

(a) COLA
(b) OWOD
(c) ECKO
(d) LIO
(e) LOW
(f) TAPE

4. This octagonal-shaped figure has its faces numbered consecutively from 1 to 8.

Imagine that it is turned anti-clockwise.

In the first move its position is changed by one face, in the second move by two faces, in the third move by three faces, and so on.

At the end of EIGHT moves what number will be in the present position of No. 1?

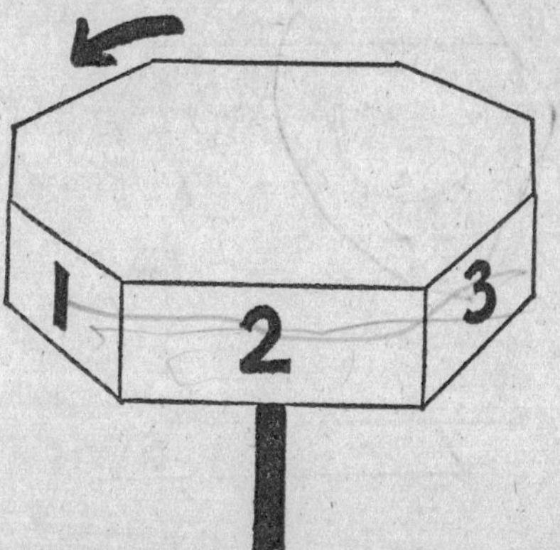

5. If MAISIE = 10 1 3 15 3 2
RUTH = 14 5 16 6
and JOAN = 7 4 1 11
What is the total of BRENDA?

6. Which is the odd face out?

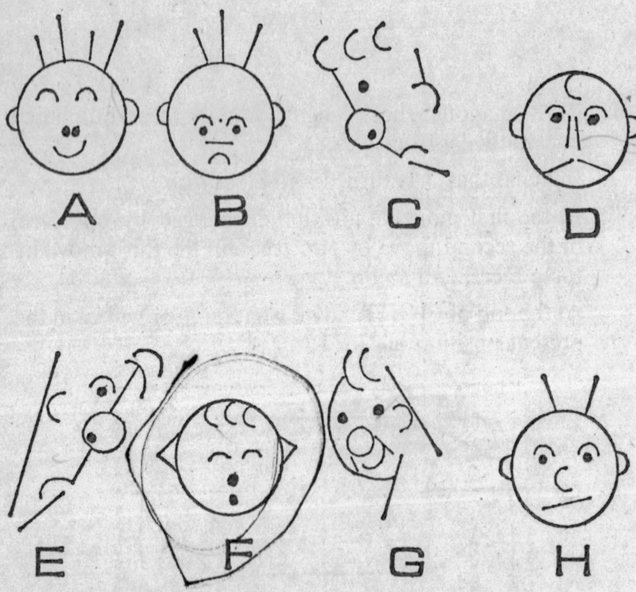

7. Which is the odd man out?

49	91	37
112	133	154

8. What are the two missing digits?

1 1 1 3 1 2 1 6 1 3 1 9 1 4 2 2 1 – 2 –

9. What should take the place of i, ii and iii?

B	E	D	C
2	i	4	3
4	25	ii	9
D	Y	iii	I

10. Which word does not conform with the others?

(a) UNFED
(b) MONMOUTH
(c) SPONSOR
(d) INDEFINITE
(e) OUTSMART

11. A word diamond here. Supply words to fit the definition given. Each word uses the letters of the previous word (not necessarily in the same order) and adds one more letter until the middle is reached. After that each word uses the letters of the previous word with one letter deducted.

	P
DAD	* *
SUITABLE	* * *
NARROW STRIP	* * * *
PARENT	* * * * *
CATCH	* * * * * *
ASSOCIATE	* * * * * * *
SURGEON'S SAW	* * * * * *
CHATTER	* * * * *
FUEL	* * * *
FAUCET	* * *
DENOTES POSITION	* *
	T

12. Which is the odd word out?

(a) DICE

(b) COUNTER

(c) CHESS-MAN

(d) DOMINO

(e) DRAUGHTSMAN

13. What numbers are represented by A, B and C?

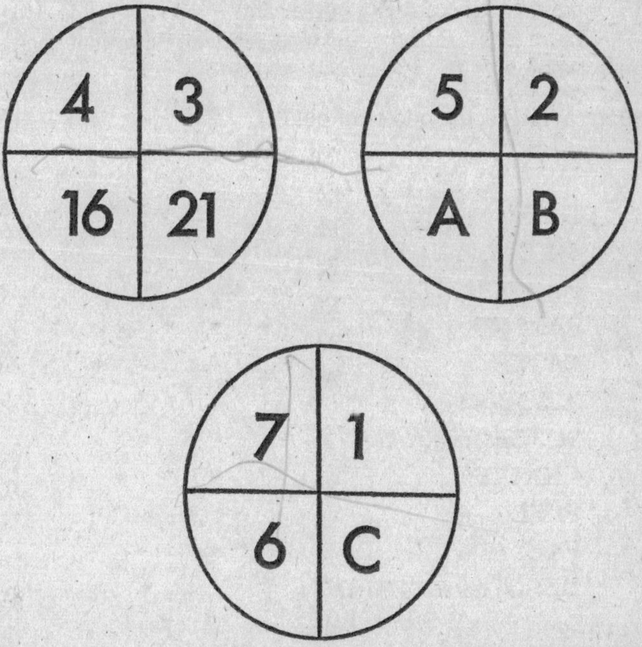

14. Three Shakespearian plays are buried away in these phrases. You must discover them by re-arranging the letters in each phrase.

1. OUR DIRT SCANDALISES
2. RUINS AT DISCOUNT
3. MEAN TO SHIFT ON

15. Which is the odd man out?

Au
Fe
Pb
Bt
Pt
Al
Ag

TEST No. 9

(Time limit: 45 minutes)

1. Which one does not conform?

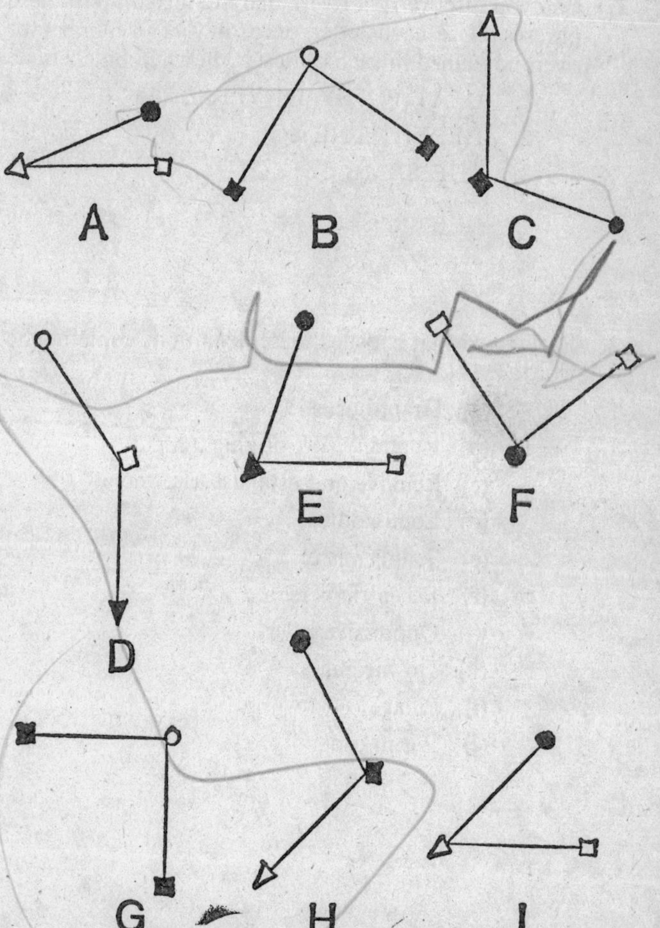

2. Can you discover the rivers that are mixed up in these phrases? Use each letter once only. The number of rivers contained in each phrase is shown in brackets.

1. NEAT POESY IN VERSE. (4)
2. HEREIN ONE SOUL. (3)
3. THE SAME SET. (2)

3. Each word that satisfies these definitions contains the word: RAN.

(a) Grain husks
(b) Roaming sort of knight?
(c) Remove and establish elsewhere
(d) Loud address
(e) Sailing vessel
(f) Eccentric person
(g) Oppressive ruler
(h) Downright
(i) Pillage
(j) Put in order

4. Examine the first four diagrams below and then decide which of the numbered diagrams at the bottom should complete the third row.

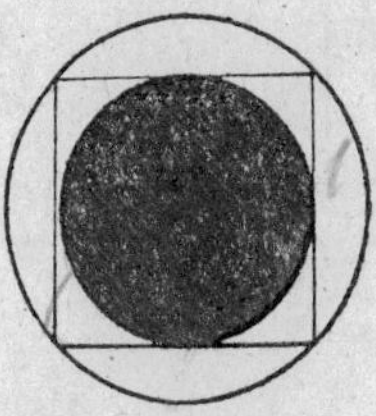

A

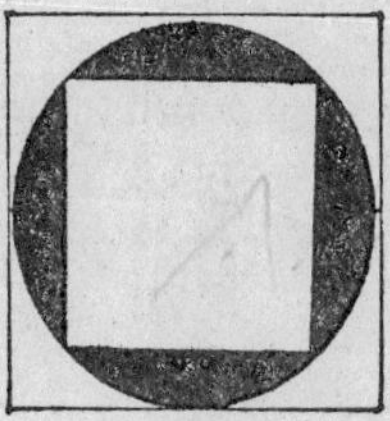

B

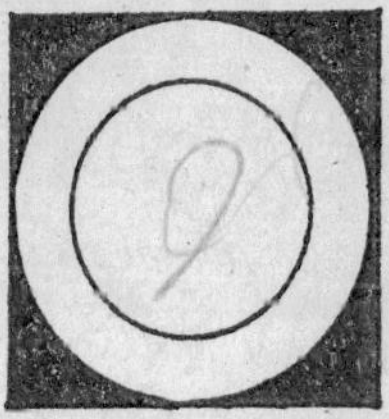

C

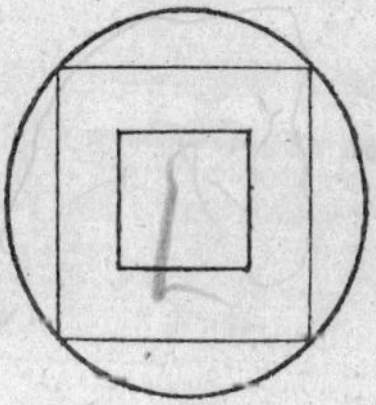

D

1 2 3 4 5

5. What numbers belong to x, y and z?

8	1	6
x	5	7
y	z	2

6. Complete this sequence:

A B C
B D E
C F I
D H O
E J W
— — —
G N S

7. Here are some football results:

ARSENAL 1 CHESTER 0
WOLVERHAMPTON 1 LIVERPOOL 2
EXETER 0 TORQUAY 0
LEEDS 1 MIDDLESBOROUGH 1
FULHAM 1 LUTON 1
HULL 2 LINCOLN 2

What were the scores in this match?

PLYMOUTH ARGYLE *v.* LEYTON?

8. Here is a new type of shorthand.

IF 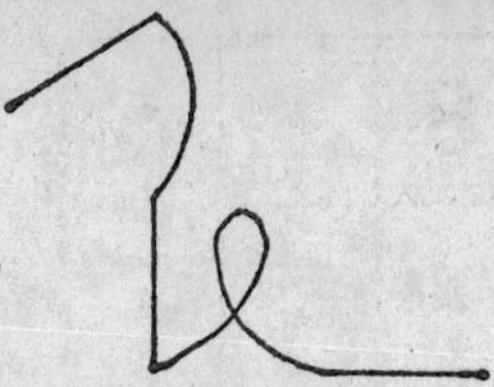 = TABLE

AND 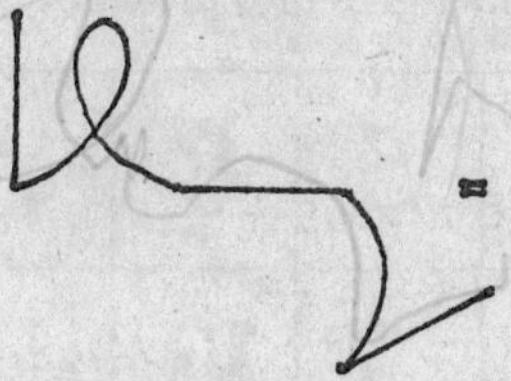 = BLEAT

WHAT ARE A AND B?

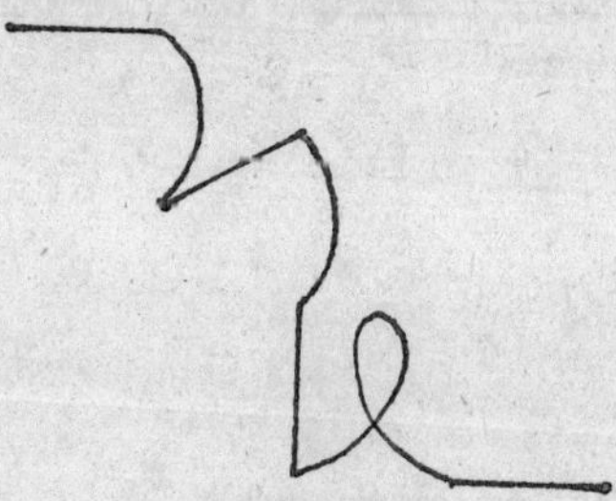

A

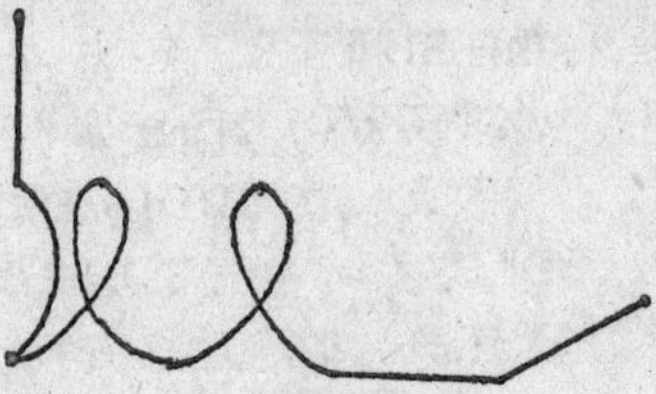

B

9. What is the next number in this sequence?

1 3 8 19 42 89 —

10. What number goes into the empty square?

0	4	5	8	7	1	3
	4	9	13		8	4

11. Which is the odd man out?

(a) CHEESE
(b) BUTTER
(c) TARRAGON
(d) SAFFRON
(e) LARD
(f) PEPPER
(g) ALLSPICE

12. What number is missing in this sequence?

4 16 8 64 32 — 512

13. Some words have different meanings which bear little relationship to each other. For example: DIVERSION can mean 'a deviation of route' or 'a pastime'. Give words which will satisfy both of the meanings shown below.

(a)	Part of ear	Block
(b)	Flock of geese	Bundle of thread
(c)	Punctuation mark	Type of butterfly
(d)	Straight edge	Sovereign
(e)	City	Money
(f)	Become wrinkled	Pouch
(g)	Game	Trifle
(h)	Short county	Plots
(i)	Coffer	Part of body
(j)	Part of body	Measure

14. Which of the numbered symbols at the bottom belongs to X?

1 6 7

14 7 8

77 98 114

4741 896 X

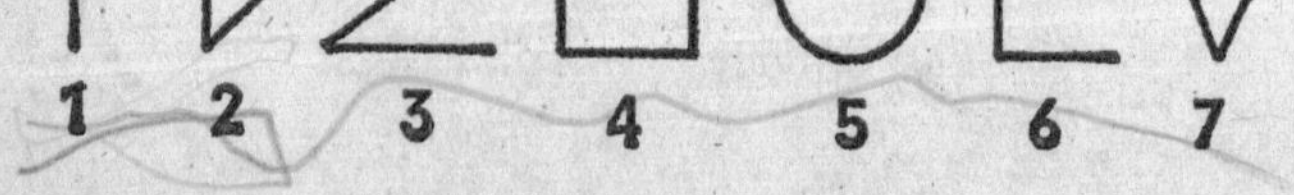

1 2 3 4 5 6 7

15. Supply the missing number:

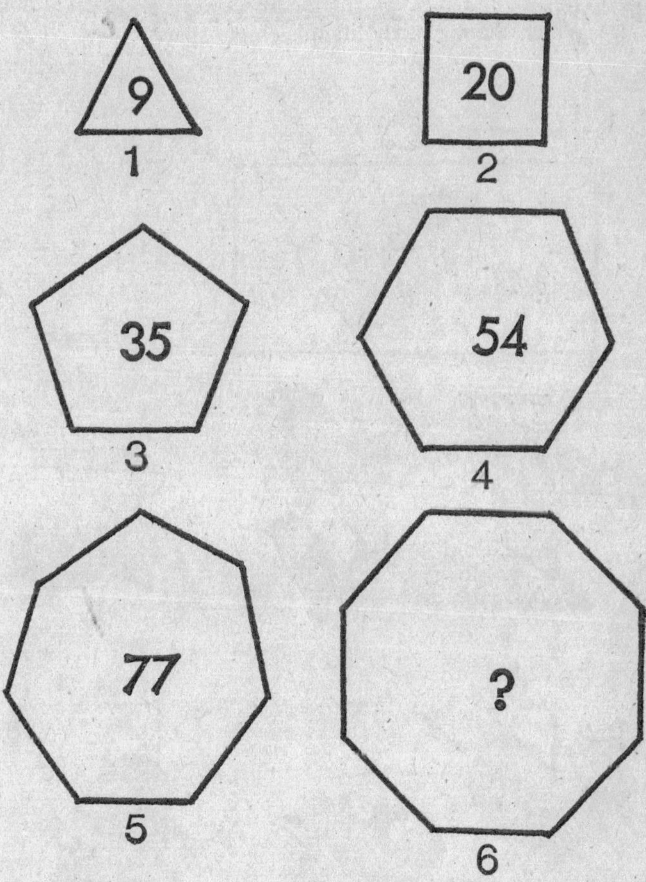

TEST No. 10

(Time limit: 45 minutes)

1. Which shape exactly fits this empty space?

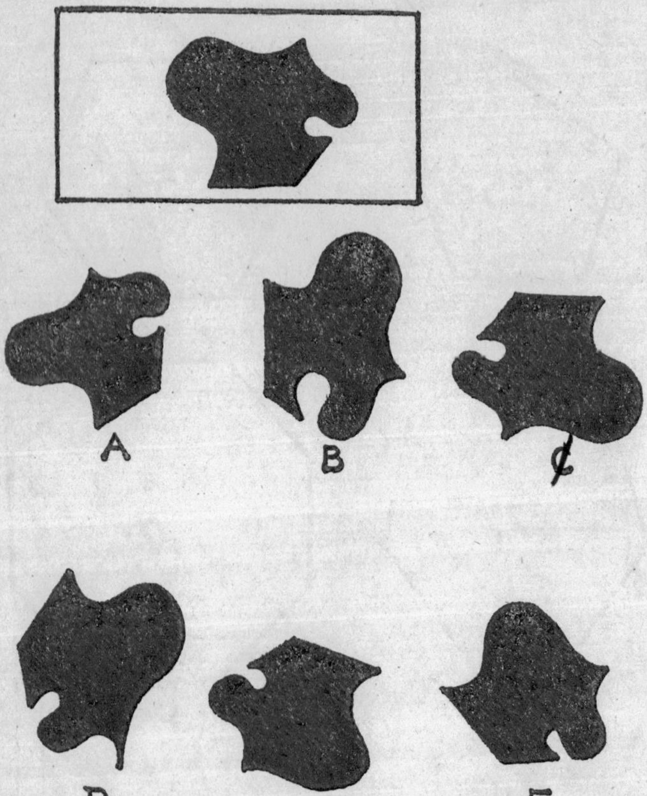

2. Which is the odd man out?

(a) RIGOLETTO
(b) LA TRAVIATA
(c) AIDA
(d) LA BOHEME
(e) LA SCALA
(f) PAGLIACCI
(g) IL TROVATORE

3. How many miles to Liverpool?

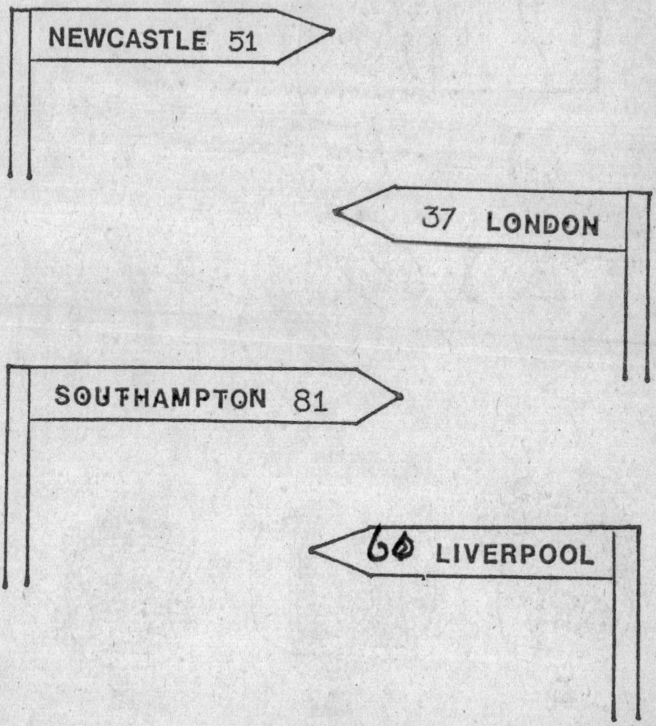

4. Which vase is wrong? 8

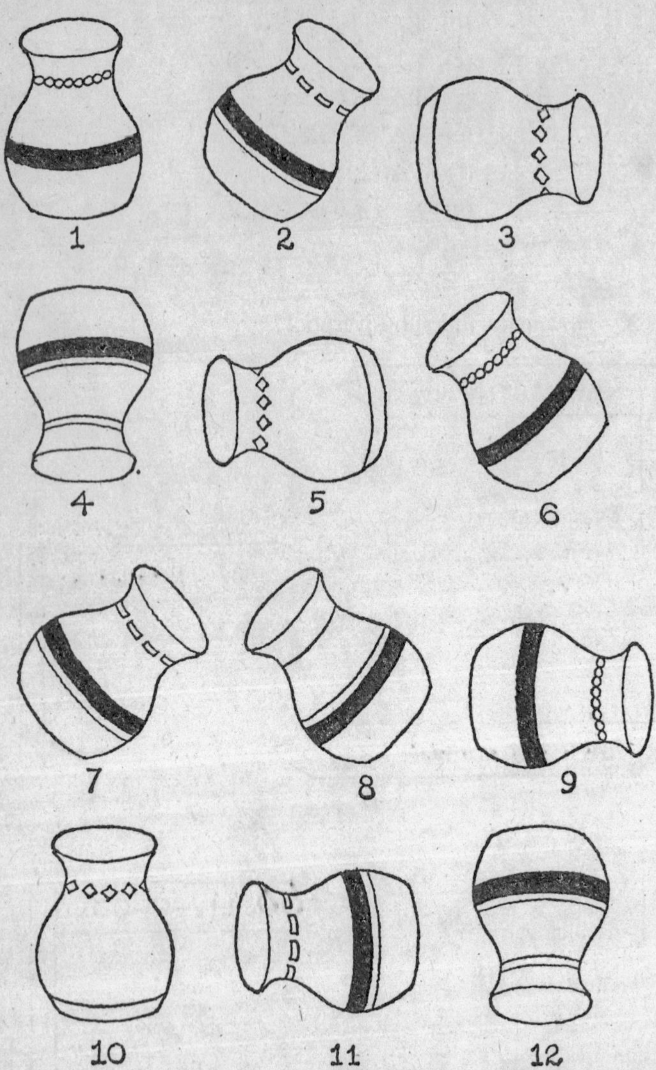

5. Change CASTOR into POLLUX in five moves, changing *two* letters each time.

```
     C A S T O R
1.   * * * * * *
2.   * * * * * *
3.   * * * * * *
4.   * * * * * *
5.   P O L L U X
```

6. Which is the odd man out?

(a) 1894
(b) 1904
(c) 1920
(d) 1914
(e) 1928
(f) 1944
(g) 1898

7. Promote SERGEANT to GENERAL. For each move you must remove one letter and arrange the rest to form a word until only one letter remains. Then ADD one letter at a time, arranging the remaining letters to form a word.

```
S E R G E A N T
 * * * * * * *
  * * * * * *
   * * * * *
    * * * *
     * * *
      * *
       *
      * *
     * * *
    * * * *
   * * * * *
  * * * * * *
 G E N E R A L
```

8. Which one is wrong?

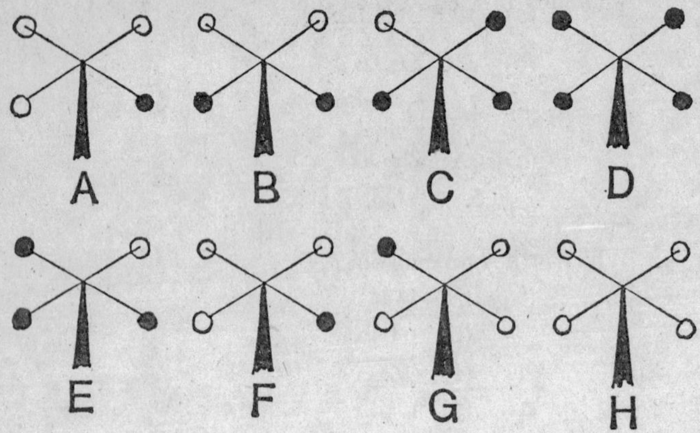

9. What should take the place of X?

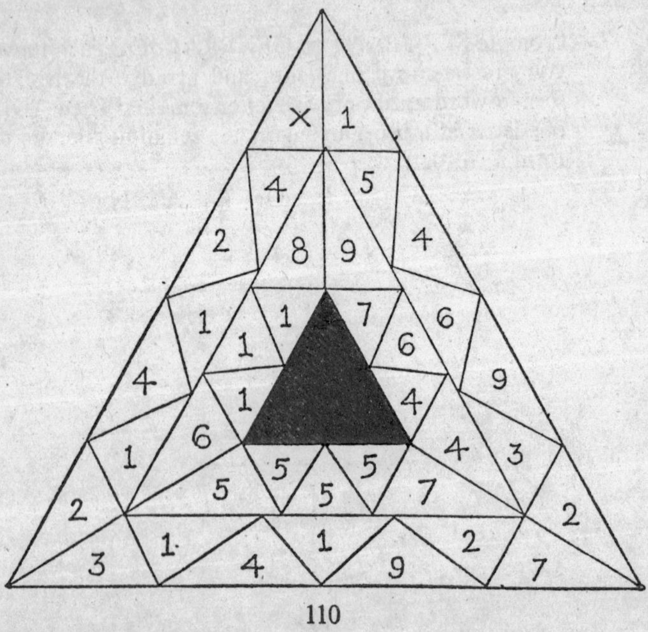

10. Which one does not belong?

(a) BAROUCHE

(b) VICTORIA

(c) LANDAU

(d) BAROQUE

(e) HANSOM

(f) GROWLER

11. What is X?

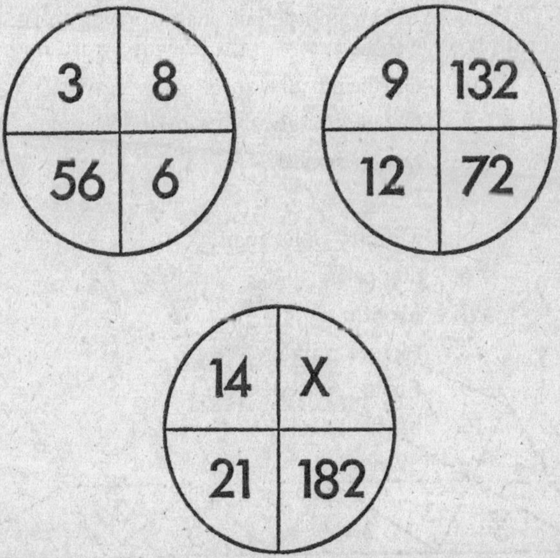

12. Here are some cricket results:

	WON	*LOST*
GLOUCESTERSHIRE	9	6
LEICESTERSHIRE	8	6
NORTHAMPTONSHIRE	11	5
NOTTINGHAMSHIRE	10	5
WORCESTERSHIRE	9	5
WARWICKSHIRE	8	4

How has CAMBRIDGESHIRE fared?

13. Each word for which definitions are given must start with the last three letters of the previous word *reversed.*

1. Glittering substance.
2. Instruction given in a period of time.
3. Quack remedy.
4. Kill.
5. Military policeman.
6. Stepped.
7. Month.
8. Picture puzzle.
9. Ersatz.
10. Musical exercise.

14. Which pattern does not conform with the others?

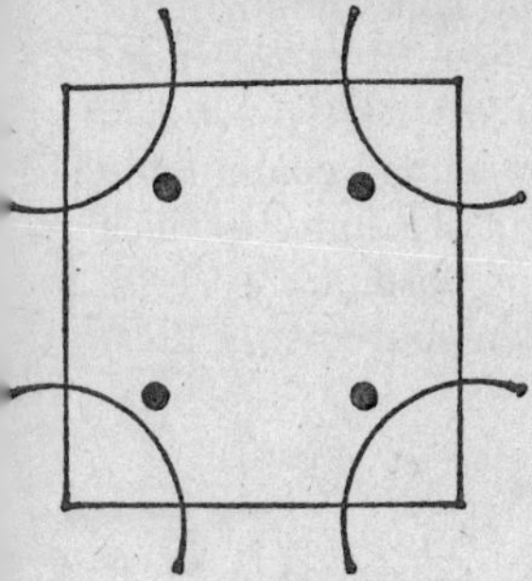

A

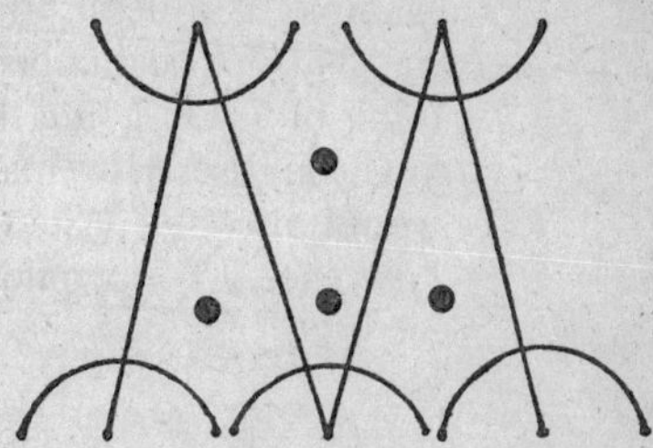

B

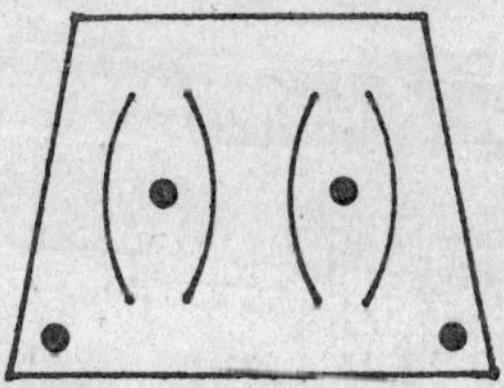

C

D

E

15. Find a number which satisfies the description shown in questions 1–10. Then discover which description given in questions a–j also satisfies that same number. For example, if a description in the first set of questions was 'No. 3. The number of days in a week', you would think of 7. On going through the second column you might find: c. 'How many Pillars of Wisdom?' – which would also be 7 ('Seven Pillars of Wisdom', by T. E. Lawrence.) You would write down your answer thus: 3 c (7).

1. How many books in the Pentateuch?
2. How many signs of the Zodiac?
3. How many sides on a British 50p piece?
4. How many spots on a die?
5. How many pounds in a quarter?
6. How many cricketers in a cricket match?
7. How many Ages of Man?
8. How many grooves on a single-sided record?
9. How many Beethoven symphonies?
10. What is the boiling-point of water in centigrade?

a. How many days in a lunar month?
b. Possession is how many points of the law?
c. How many apostles?
d. The number of deadly sins?
e. How many five-pound notes make a 'pony'?
f. How many metres in a hectometre?
g. How many wonders of the world?
h. How many eyes had Cyclops?
i. How many yards in a chain?
j. How many points in a game of table tennis?

ANSWERS

TEST No. 6

1. (a) For BEAR ance
(b) PIG ment
(c) S CAT he
(d) B ASS oon (or COW - bell)
(e) A MULE t
(f) Stal LION
(g) DOG matic
(h) STAG nate
(i) Comman DEER
(j) E BULL ient
(Score 1 point for each correct answer. Maximum: 10 points)

2. X = 6
Y = 36
X is the product of the top two numbers and
Y is the square of X.
(1 point, but X and Y must both be correct)

3. (c)! Does this surprise you? Whereas (a) and (b) each contain ALL the letters of the alphabet, (c) does not. (a) and (b) were the invention of your inquisitor and are therefore quite unfamiliar to you. Many people know the sentence: 'The quick brown fox jumps over the lazy dog', which *does* contain all the letters of the alphabet, and is often used to test a typewriter. These people may have immediately assumed that (c) contained all the letters of the alphabet, but closer examination reveals that I have changed JUMPS to JUMPED, with the result that the sentence does not contain the letter 'S'. **(2 points)**

4. 

In the top row the three digits at the top decrease by 1 in each circle, while the three digits underneath increase by 1 each time.

In the middle row the three letters at the top decrease by 1 in each circle, while the letters underneath increase by 1 each time.

Following this same pattern, therefore, in the bottom row, in which letters and digits are mixed together, those at the top decrease by 1 each time, while those underneath increase by 1 each time.
(2 points, but only if all correct)

5. No. 1. Each row will then contain:

   (i) A scalene triangle (one with unequal sides);

   (ii) A right-angled triangle – which is at present missing from the second row;

   (iii) An isosceles triangle (one with two equal sides);

(iv) An equilateral triangle (one with all sides equal).

(3 points)

6. (a) AUSTRALIA. The letters have been advanced one place in their alphabetic order.

(b) INDIA. The letters have been advanced two places in their alphabetic order.

(c) GREECE. The letters go back one place in their alphabetic order.

(Score 1 point for each correct country. Maximum: 3 points)

7. DOZEN

NEIGHBOUR

RURAL

LATIN

NIL

LITRE

ERROR

ROUEN

NEWT

TWENTY

(Score 1 point for 5 or more correct; 2 points if all correct)

8. (i) Globe A

(ii) Globe G

The globes are rotating anti-clockwise.

In (i) there are two vertical rows of spots situated

adjacent to each other. At X one of these rows (the centre one on the first globe) will be on the blind side and only one row will be visible.

In (ii) there are three vertical rows of spots on one side of the globe only. On the other side there are no spots. Therefore at Y there will be one row visible, while in the next position of the globe all three rows will be on the blind side.

(1 point for each correct answer. Maximum: 2 points)

9. (b) PHILEMON, which is in the New Testament. All the others are in the Old Testament. **(2 points)**

10. 22, 286

Alternate numbers, starting at 7, advance by 4, 5 and 6. The alternate numbers starting at 91 are thirteen times the previous number.

(1 point for each. Maximum: 2 points)

11. F. The figure rotates $\frac{1}{4}$ turn anti-clockwise. The difference in shading remains constant throughout. In F the small outer circle and the triangle have changed places. **(Score 2 points)**

12. B. **(1 point)**

13. The treble recorder, which should not have the mouthpiece of the bassoon.

The trumpet, which should have three pistons, and not four, as shown.

The violin, because the sound holes are the wrong way round.

(I'm sorry about the piano! Did you mark it as wrong because it has three pedals? In fact many pianos –

especially grand pianos – *do* have three pedals.)
(Score 1 point for each correct answer. Maximum: 3 points. *But deduct one point if you have marked any of the others as being wrong.*)

14.	PUMA	or	PUMA	or any
1.	PUMP		PUMP	other
2.	PULP		POMP	variation,
3.	PULL		ROMP	provided
4.	POLL		ROME	each word
5.	POLE		ROLE	is genuine.
6.	VOLE		VOLE	

(Score 2 points, but only if all correct)

15. (a) KERRY, which is in Ireland, the others being in the U.S.A. **(1 point)**

TEST No. 7

1. (A) = 7
(B) = 8
From the music shown the following can be deduced:

after  comes 

after  comes 

after  comes 

after 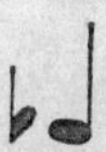 comes

Therefore, (A) must be  , following 

and (B) must be  , following 

(Score 1 point for each. Maximum: 2 points)

2. A = 9

   B = 2

   The first row across totals 15; the second row 16; the fifth row 19 and the bottom row 20. Thus, the total increases by one in each successive row.
   (Score 1 point for each. Maximum: 2 points)

3. Y.

   There are four strokes making up the first letter in each row; three strokes make the second letter, and two strokes SHOULD make the third letter. (There are three strokes in the letter Y.) **(2 points)**

4. (e) CAT'S CRADLE, which is a game. The others are knots. **(1 point)**

5. 1.

   The shapes are moved progressively upwards, the top shape becoming the bottom shape with each move. The top row indicates the manner in which the black and white shapes are varied. and the bottom row conforms to this, except that black takes the place of white and vice versa. **(2 points)**

6. A. **(2 points)**

   Did you think of holding the page up to the light and studying it from the reverse side? It might have helped.

7. (a) RAMPART
(b) PARTAKE
(c) REPARTEE
(d) APARTMENT
(e) PARTRIDGE
(f) PARTIAL
(g) PARTICLE
(h) PARTNER
(i) DEPARTMENT
(j) IMPART

If you selected PART for (g) PORTION, count it as correct.
(Score 1 point for each word. Maximum: 10 points)

8. (h) FRANCE, which only contains two vowels. All the other words contain three. If you were thinking in terms of the actual countries (e.g. Africa is a continent), the clue was given in the question: 'Which is the odd WORD out?' **(2 points)**

9. 6,561. There are two sequences arranged alternately. In each sequence the number is the square of the previous number *in that sequence.* 6,561 is the square of 81. **(2 points)**

10. A. **(1 point)**

11. (d) EMPEROR, which is a piano concerto (or even a waltz). All the others are symphonies. **(1 point)**

12. APPREHEND, MINE, SCALE, PUMP, SET, LETTER, STAFF, BYPASS.
(Score 1 point for each correct word. Maximum: 8 points)

13. (d) ACCORDING. (All the other words have *either* the vowels or the consonants in alphabetic order.) **(Score 2 points)**

14. (a) $\frac{1}{2}$ revolution.

(b) $2\frac{1}{2}$ revolutions.

(Score 1 point for each. Maximum: 2 points)

15. E. The light should be in the lower glass, since, when the signal-arm goes up there will be no light showing. **(2 points)**

TEST No. 8

1. (a) Twang

(b) Wand

(c) Rowan

(d) Wander

(e) Swank

(f) Wane

(g) Want

(h) Wanton

(i) Swan

(j) Gowan

(Score 1 point for each correct word. Maximum: 10 points)

2. X = 840

Y = 168

Z = 24

Values of the shapes as indicated are: square = 4, circle = 5, and triangle = 6. The value of the rectangle is not indicated, but is obviously 7. This is ascertained from the relationship between 4 (square) and 28, or 5 (circle) and 35. From this it can also be seen that the values of overlapping areas are obtained by multiplying the values of the individual shapes that make up those areas.

Confirmation of this is given by 140, which is the product of 4, 5 and 7.

Therefore, X is the product of the circle, square, triangle and rectangle; Y is the product of the triangle, rectangle and square; Z is the product of the triangle and square.

(Score 2 points for each correct answer; maximum: 6 points)

3. (e).

All the other words are anagrams of types of fuel. (a) COAL; (b) WOOD; (c) COKE; (d) OIL; (f) PEAT. The only anagram of (e) is OWL, which is not a fuel.
(Score 1 point)

4. 5. **(Score 5 points)**

5. 32.

The vowels are valued as follows:

A=1 E=2 I=3 O=4 U=5

The consonants are valued according to their order in the alphabet *when the vowels are omitted.* Thus, BRENDA becomes

1 14 2 11 3 1

making a total of 32.
(Score 3 points)

6. H.

The faces are made up of four straight lines, five curves, two dots and one circle. In H there are only three straight lines. **(Score 2 points)**

7. 37.

All the others are divisible by seven. **(2 points)**

8. 5 and 5.

Here the spacing may have confused you. Had the digits been placed as follows:

11 13 12 16 13 19 14 22 15 25

you would probably have recognised that there were two alternate sequences, one ascending 1 at a time (11, 12, 13, 14, 15) and the other ascending 3 at a time (13, 16, 19, 22, 25).
(Score 2 points for each. Maximum: 4 points)

9. (i)=5 (ii)=16 (iii)=P

The second row across shows the order in the alphabet of the letters in the first row.
In the third row the numbers in the second row are squared.
In the bottom row letters are substituted for the order in the alphabet shown in the third row.
(Score 1 point for each correct. Maximum: 3 points)

10. (d) INDEFINITE.

All the other words contain three consecutive letters *in reverse order* (unFED, mONMouth, sPONsor, oUTSmart) whereas INDEFINITE contains three consecutive letters in the correct order – inDEFinite.
(2 points)

11.

```
            P
          P   A
        A   P   T
      T   A   P   E
    P   A   T   E   R
  E   N   T   R   A   P
P   A   R   T   N   E   R
  T   R   E   P   A   N
    P   R   A   T   E
      P   E   A   T
        T   A   P
          A   T
            T
```

(Score 1 point for 7 or more correct; 2 points if all correct. Maximum: 2 points)

12. (a) DICE, which is plural. All the other words are singular. **(2 points)**

13. A=11 B=26 C=36

Examination of the numbers given shows that each number is obtained by multiplying the opposite lower number by five and adding one. In the first circle 5 times 3+1=16 and 5 times 4+1=21. In the third circle 5 times 1+1=6.

(Score 1 point for each. Maximum: 3 points)

14. 1. TROILUS AND CRESSIDA

2. TITUS ANDRONICUS

3. TIMON OF ATHENS

(Score 1 point for each correct answer. Maximum: 3 points)

15. Bt., which is an abbreviation for 'baronet'. The others are chemical symbols denoting the following metals: Au=gold (aurum); Fe=iron (ferrum); Pb=lead (plumbum); Pt=platinum; Al=aluminium; Ag=silver (argentum). **(Score 5 points)**

TEST No. 9

1. E.

Acute angles have symbols at the end of the lines, as shown in the first row. Obtuse angles and right angles have different symbols.

In the second row the colours of the symbols are reversed (black becoming white and white becoming black), and in the third row they are reversed again.

Therefore, in E the circle and square are the wrong colours. **(2 points)**

2. 1. SEINE, PO, SEVERN, TAY

2. OUSE, RHONE, NILE

3. THAMES, TEES

(Score 1 point for each river. Maximum: 9 points)

3. (a) BRAN

(b) ERRANT

(c) TRANSPLANT

(d) HARANGUE

(e) CATAMARAN

(f) CRANK

(g) TYRANT

(h) ARRANT

(i) RANSACK

(j) ARRANGE

(Score 1 point for each word correct. Maximum: 10 points)

4. 4.

A, B, C and D are made up of circles and squares.

In A there is a circle inside a square inside a circle;

in B there is a square inside a circle inside a square;

in C there is a circle inside a circle inside a square;

in D there is a square inside a square inside a circle.

The third row is made up of triangles and circles, conforming in the same way.

In A the centre figure (the circle) is black; in B the middle figure (the circle) is black; in C the outer figure (the square) is black; in D none of the figures is black. The third row must conform in the same way.

(Score 3 points)

5. x = 3

y = 4

z = 9

The total of each line, horizontally, vertically and diagonally, will then be fifteen.

(Score 1 point, but only if all correct)

6. F L G.

The first letter (reading downwards) advances one place each move; the second letter advances two places each move; the third letter advances two, then four, then six, then eight places. Therefore W is advanced ten places (reverting to A when Z is reached).

(Score 3 points)

7. PLYMOUTH ARGYLE 2   LEYTON 1

Score one goal for each L in the name of the team. **(Score 3 points)**

8. A = EATABLE

B = BALLET

Examination of the two words given reveals the following:

(Score 2 points for each correct word. Maximum: 4 points)

9. 184.

Double the first number and add 1;

double the second number and add 2;

double the third number and add 3.

Continuing in this manner:

double the sixth number (89) and add six. **(Score 3 points)**

10. 15.

The lower number is the sum of the number above it and its preceding number. **(Score 2 points)**

11. (e) LARD.

All the other words contain double letters: chEEse, buTTer, taRRagon; saFFron, pePPer, aLLspice. **(Score 2 points)**

12. 1,024.

The first number is squared to give the second number, which is then halved to give the third number. This in turn is squared to give the next number, and so on. **(Score 1 point)**

13.
(a) ANVIL
(b) SKEIN
(c) COMMA
(d) RULER
(e) CAPITAL
(f) PURSE
(g) BAGATELLE
(h) BEDS
(i) CHEST
(j) FOOT

(Score 1 point for each correct word. Maximum: 10 points)

14. No. 2.

In the first row there is one horizontal line (in the 7), one vertical line (in the 1), one diagonal line (in the 7) and one circle (in the 6).

In the second line there are two of each.

In the third line there are three of each.

In the fourth line there should be four of each.

There ARE four circles (in 896), but only three vertical, horizontal and diagonal lines. No. 2 is the only figure which supplies all three. **(Score 4 points)**

15. 104.

Divide the number inside the shape by the number of

sides of the shape. Thus, 9 divided by 3 (sides of the triangle) gives 3; 20 divided by 4 (sides of the square) gives 5, and so on. You then arrive at the progression: 3, 5, 7, 9, 11 and 13. Therefore, in No. 6, which is an octagon, the number inside should be 104 which, divided by 8, gives 13 – the final number of the progression. **(Score 3 points)**

TEST No. 10

1. C. **(1 point)**

2. (e) LA SCALA – an opera house. The rest are operas. **(1 point)**

3. 62 miles.

   In each town you must find the order in the alphabet of each letter, add them together and halve the result. Thus: L=12, I=9, V=22, E=5, R=18, P=16, O=15, O=15, L=12. Total: 124, which halved, gives 62. **(3 points)**

4. No. 8.

   A vase with a broad black band round the centre has a row of circles round its neck; if there is a broad black band with a thin line below it round the centre, there is a row of rectangles round the neck; if there is a thin line near the bottom of the vase there is a row of diamonds round the neck.
   When there is a broad black band round the centre with a thin line above it there should be a double line going round the neck, but in No. 8 there is only a single line. **(Score 2 points)**

5. CASTOR
1. MASTER
2. MATTED
3. POTTED
4. POLLED
5. POLLUX

You may have completed this word-change using different words. If so, and provided all the words are genuine, score points. **(Score 3 points, but only if completed)**

6. (d) 1914, which was *not* a leap year. In a leap year the last *two* figures must be divisible by four. As 14 is not divisible by four, it was not a leap year (1916 was the next leap year). **(1 point)**

7. S E R G E A N T
R E A G E N T
G A R N E T
G R E A T
T E A R
A R T
A T
A
R A
R A G
G E A R
A G R E E
E N R A G E
G E N E R A L

(Score 1 point for first half completed; 1 point for second half completed. Maximum: 2 points)
(Alternative words will count, as long as they are genuine)

8. F.

In the first row the balls are arranged as follows:

A: 1 black ball; B: 2 black balls; C: 3 black balls; D: 4 black balls.

In the second row the WHITE balls should follow the same arrangement, so that F should have two white balls instead of three. **(1 point)**

9. 3.

The total of the numbers on each side of the large triangle should be the same as the total on the same side of the small triangle. The total of the numbers on the left-hand side of the small triangle is 17, made up of 8, 1, 1, 1, and 6. The numbers given on the side of the large triangle are 2, 1, 4, 1, 2, and 4, giving a total of 14. Therefore the remaining number must be 3, to bring the total up to 17. **(2 points)**

10. (d) BAROQUE, which means 'grotesque'. The others are carriages. **(1 point)**

11. X = 420.

Opposite numbers are obtained by multiplying the smaller number by one less than itself. In the first circle: 3 multiplied by 2 gives 6 and 8 multiplied by 7 gives 56; in the second circle 9 multiplied by 8 gives 72 and 12 multiplied by 11 gives 132. In the third circle 14 multiplied by 13 gives 182 and 21 multiplied by 20 gives 420. **(2 points)**

12. CAMBRIDGESHIRE WON 9 and LOST 5.

The number of wins in each case is the number of consonants in the name and the number of losses is the number of vowels. **(2 points)**

13. TinSEL, LESSON, NOStRUM, MURDER, RED-CAP, PACED, DECemBER, REBUS, SUBstitUTE, ETUde.
(Score 1 point for each word correct. Maximum: 10 points)

14. B.

Each pattern consists of four straight lines, four curves and four dots, except B, which has five curves. **(1 point)**

15. 1 e (5)
2 c (12)
3 d (7) OR 3 g (7)
4 j (21)
5 a (28)
6 i (22)
7 d (7) OR 7 g (7)
8 h (1) (!) (There is only one groove in a single-sided record.)
9 b (9)
10 f (100)
(Score 1 point for each correct answer. Maximum: 10 points)

GROUP II

Ratings for Tests 6–10

The total score possible for these tests is 234 points made up as follows:

TEST No. 6	38 points
TEST No. 7	41 points
TEST No. 8	53 points
TEST No. 9	60 points
TEST No. 10	42 points

Points are only scored for answers given within the specified time limits.

A score of 180 or over is excellent, and shows that you are well on the way to solving the remaining problems in Group III.

155–180 is very good, and it is possible that you were handicapped mainly by the time limits imposed. No doubt, given more time, you would have recorded an even higher score. Perhaps you could improve your vocabulary.

130–155 is still good in view of the more difficult nature of the problems and the time limits.

100–130 is the average score, so if you are within this range there is no reason to feel inferior about your aptitude.

75–100 is not bad, but you should go over all the problems again, referring to the answers in order to ascertain the reasoning that has gone into them.

Under 75. You should have gained something by attempting

to solve them, but it appears that you have not yet mastered the technique of these tests. Aim for a better understanding of the meanings of words. However, have a go at the problems in Group III. You may do better than you expect.

GROUP III

TESTS 11–14

Difficult

Reasoning and deduction	46%
Vocabulary	29%
Numerical	17%
Knowledge	5%
Visuo-spatial	2%
Visual perception	1%

TEST No. 11

(Time limit: 65 minutes)

1. To continue this sequence, which figure should be repeated after No. 8?

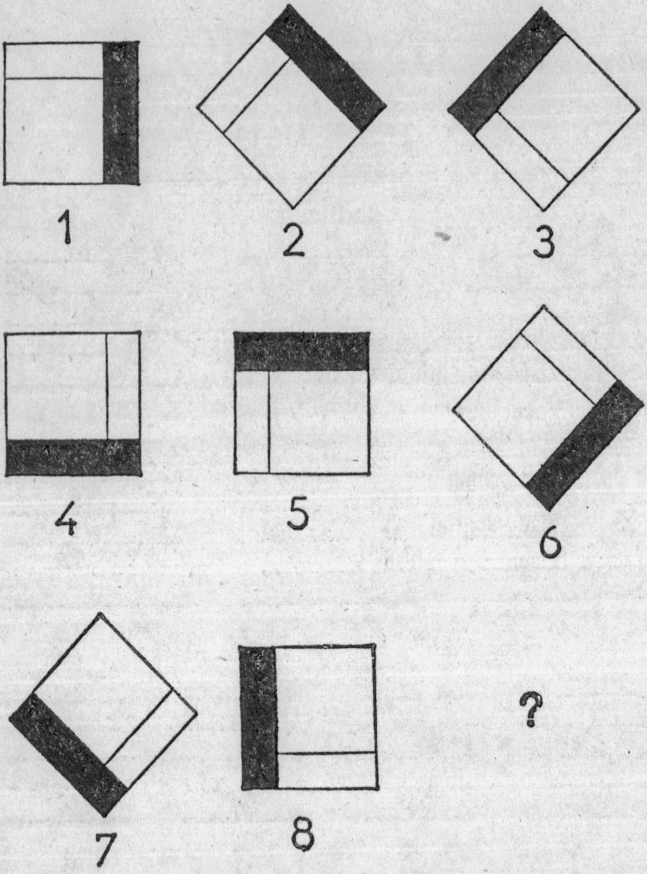

2. A shopkeeper had very little space in his crowded shop and the scales on his counter took up a lot of room which he could ill afford.

Realising that everything he sold was weighed in pounds, and that the heaviest article weighed 40 lbs., he decided to economise on space by using four weights only.

With these four weights he was able to weigh anything from 1 lb. to 40 lbs. inclusive.

What were the four weights?

3. Which of the bottom figures will complete F?

4. Complete the following words, using all the letters of these words (using each letter once only).

SISTER REALISED
DETEST PERMISSION

```
C A N * * * * *
* C A N * * * *
* * C A N * * *
* * * C A N * *
* * * * C A N *
* * * * * C A N
```

5. Complete this sequence:

9 3 16 4 25 5 – –

6. What number must be placed in the brackets?

CAT (2) DOG

PIG (0) RAM

COW ( ) GNU

7. What are the values of A and B?

= 17

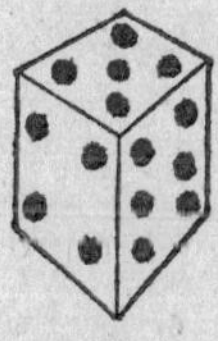

= 10

= 12

= 3

= 9

= 9

= A?

= B?

8. Which of these words are mis-spelt?

(a) EISTEDDFOD
(b) DESSICATE
(c) ACCELLERATE
(d) DIAPHRAGM
(e) SIEGE
(f) OSCILLATE
(g) INUENDO
(h) INNOCULATE
(i) IMPENETRIBLE
(j) PNEUMONIA

9. Which is the intruder?

(a) TURNIP
(b) LUPIN
(c) LILAC
(d) PEAR
(e) APPLE
(f) MARROW

10. Which of these fractions is out of place?

$\frac{2}{8}$ $\frac{5}{25}$ $\frac{4}{64}$ $\frac{6}{216}$

$\frac{7}{343}$ $\frac{3}{27}$

11. Which of the numbered figures at the bottom should take the place of X?

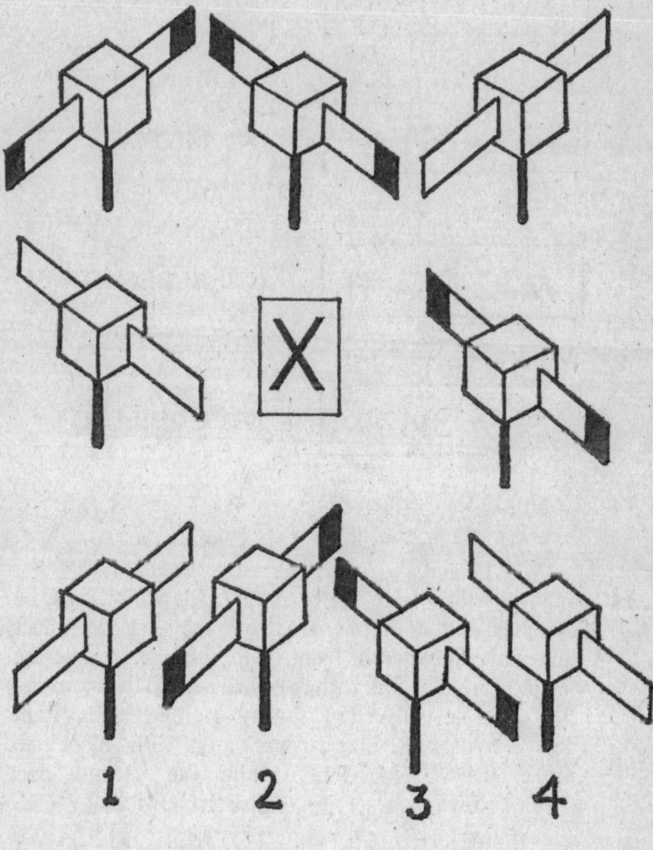

12. In these car number-plates the last letter indicates the year of registration, M being used for 1974, L for 1973, and so forth, working backwards. The letter 'I', however, was not used.

What is the number-plate for a 1966 DAF?

XUJ 385 G	1969 CHEVROLET
HKL 691 L	1973 FIAT
MJO 254 H	1970 BEDFORD
XLO 314 J	1971 CADILLAC

13. Complete this sequence:

2 3 8 * 3968

14. What words go into the brackets? The words must be two-syliabled or hyphenated and the first part must link with the word in front of the brackets, while the second part must link with the word behind the brackets. For example: BLACK (BOARD-ROOM) SERVICE. The first part of 'Board-room' links with 'black', to make 'BLACKBOARD', while the second part ('room') links with 'service' to give 'ROOM SERVICE'.

BLACK (. . . . . .) CLOTHES (. . . . .)
HORN (. . . .) MEETING (. . . . .)
RAY (. . . . .) ROOM

15. Give values for x, y and z.

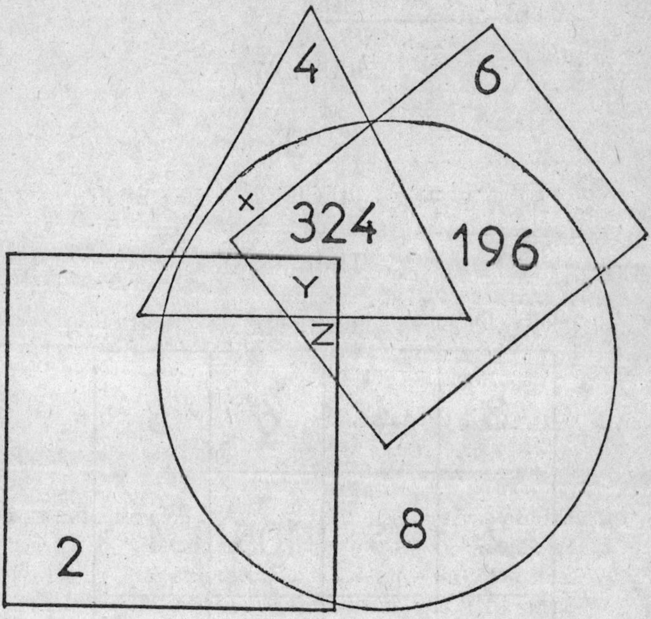

TEST No. 12

(Time limit: 75 minutes)

1. Find a word for each space which makes a common link between the previous and the following word.

For example: house (BOAT) swain.

FREE

. . . .

BARROW

. . . .

SCOUT

. . . .

PIECE

. . . .

TIME

2. What is the missing number?

3	4	6	5
2	15	105	4
7	480		8
8	9	6	7

3. There is a fallacy in this story.
Read it through carefully and see if you can spot what is wrong with it.

> An engaged couple went to their vicar and told him they wanted to get married as soon as possible. The vicar explained that the banns would have to be published on three successive Sundays, after which the marriage could take place.
> 'That will suit us fine,' they said. 'We would like you to marry us on the Saturday following the final reading of the banns.'
> The vicar consulted his book.
> 'I'm afraid that will be impossible,' he said. 'It so happens that I have an unusually busy day already on that Saturday. I have four weddings, two christenings and a funeral, and it's impossible to get anything else in. I could marry you a week later on the following Saturday.'
> Reluctantly, the couple agreed.

4. Continue this sequence:

2 2 2 4 5 3 16 8 4 – – –

5. Complete this series:

LI CLIII —— MCCCLXXVII

6. Pair words in the first column with words in the second column. For example: HORSE – POWER.

PAR	TREE
NOT	BOX
SPEAR	ICE
CHRISTMAS	SIDE
PIN	PEN
OFF	HEAD
ICE	SON
FOUNTAIN	NET
SON	ROT
HORSE	RINK
CAR	MINT

7. What term will continue this sequence?

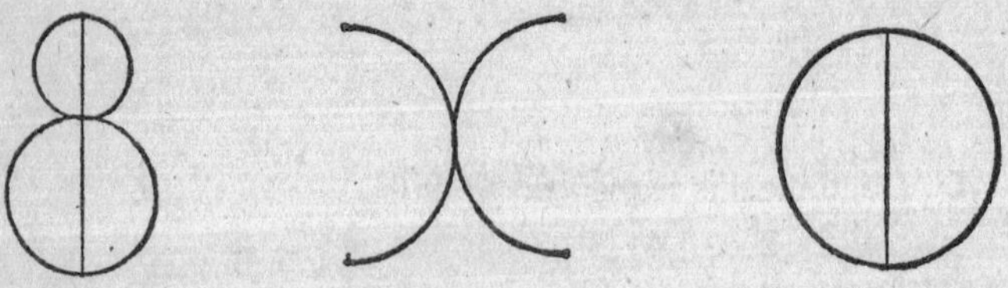

8. Decode this message:

FOFNZ CVVCEM
DWODBSDC RMKMPPMU

9. Which figure is wrong?

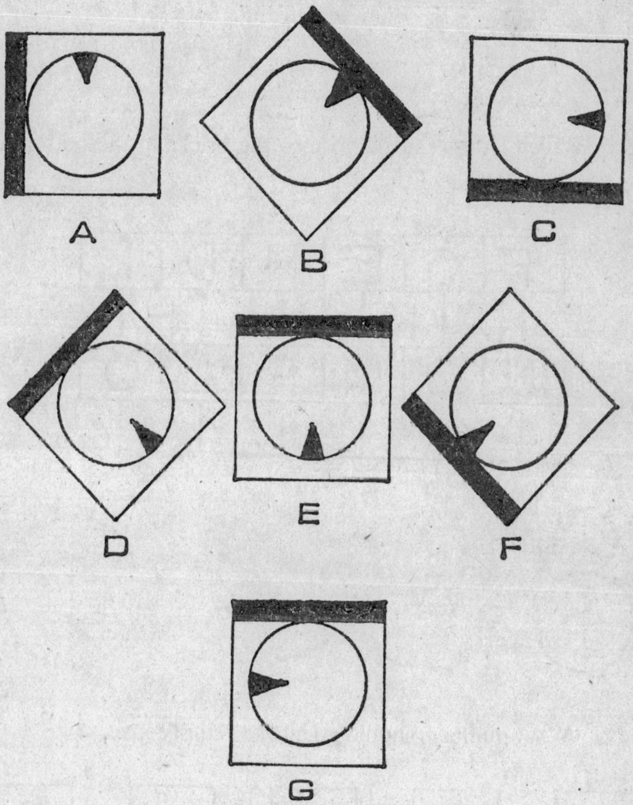

10. What three numbers will continue this sequence?

2 3 4 4 9 16 16 81 256 – – –

11. Which letters should go into the bricks in the bottom line?

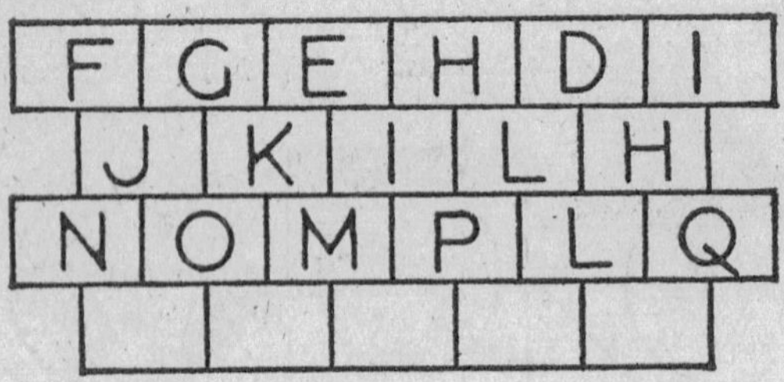

12. What numbers should go into the empty spaces?

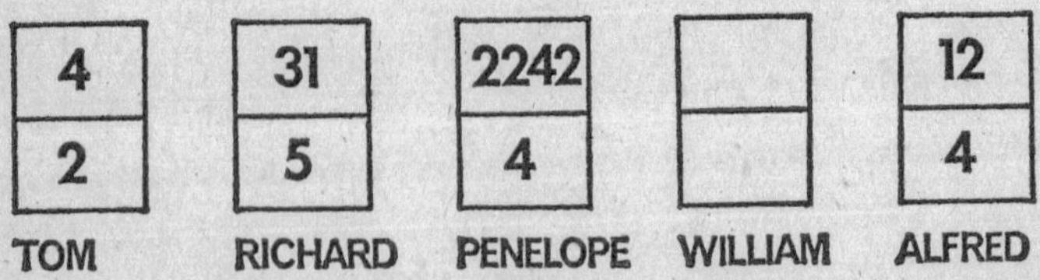

13. Arrange these words in the form of a word-square.

IRIS	ELSE	REIN	DENE
REEL	ACRE	CERE	ARID

14. These were the scores as the wickets fell in a cricket match.

57	74	89	108	121	142	153	176	185
1	2	3	4	5	6	7	8	9

What was the final score?

15. Complete this sequence:

1 7 3 2 6 5 3 – 7 4 4

TEST No. 13

(Time limit: 75 minutes)

1. There is a fallacy in this story.
Read it carefully and see if you can see what is wrong with it.

> On a hot summer's day last December in Durban a woman lay asleep on the *chaise longue* on the stoep of her bungalow.
> She was lying on her side and having a vivid dream.
> She dreamed that she was living in 1793, during the French Revolution, and had been captured by Robespierre.
> Accused of being associated with his rivals, the Girondins, she was sentenced to be guillotined.
> In her dream she placed her head in the guillotine and awaited the dreaded fall of the blade.
> Just as it was rushing down, her husband, who had come out onto the stoep, touched her on the back of the neck to wake her.
> The shock of this, coinciding, as it did, exactly with the critical moment in her dream, killed her instantly.

2. Here is a sentence in which all the vowels have been removed.
You have to insert vowels so as to make sense of it.

H L F L F S B T T R T H N N B R D

3. Which cards belong to:

(a) ELIZABETH?

(b) TOM?

(c) PAMELA?

(d) ARTHUR?

PHILIP

PENELOPE

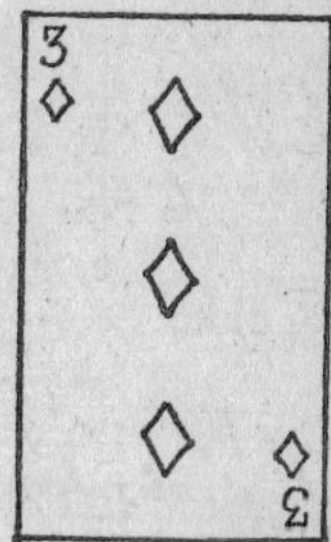

ANN

EDGAR

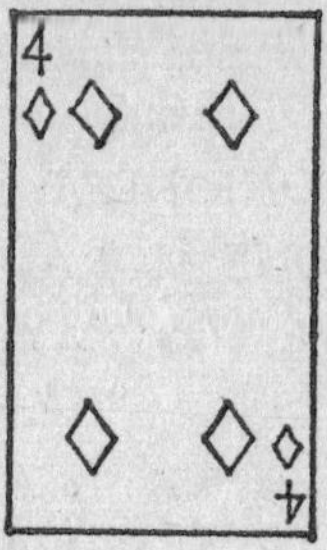

IRIS

WILLIAM

4. What numbers should go into D?

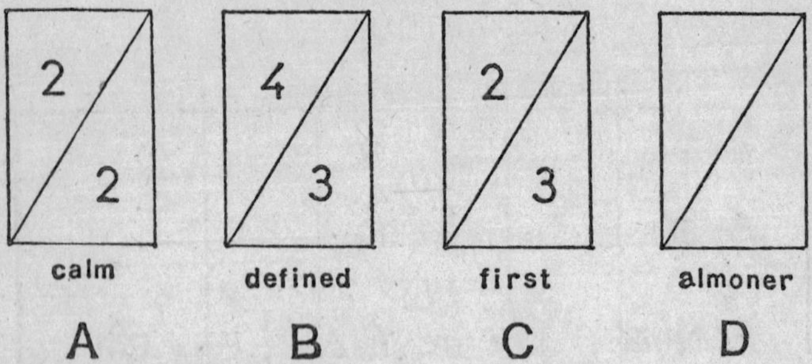

5. Can you pick the flowers?
Each sentence below contains two or three flowers, though you'll need to be good at flower-arrangement to find them.
The number of flowers is shown in brackets, and you must use each letter once only.

A. YES, ONE DROP, I SAY. (3)
B. DIG ONE MORAL NAME. (2)
C. O, I'VE LOST MY REAR! (2)

6. Supply answers to A and B.

(A)

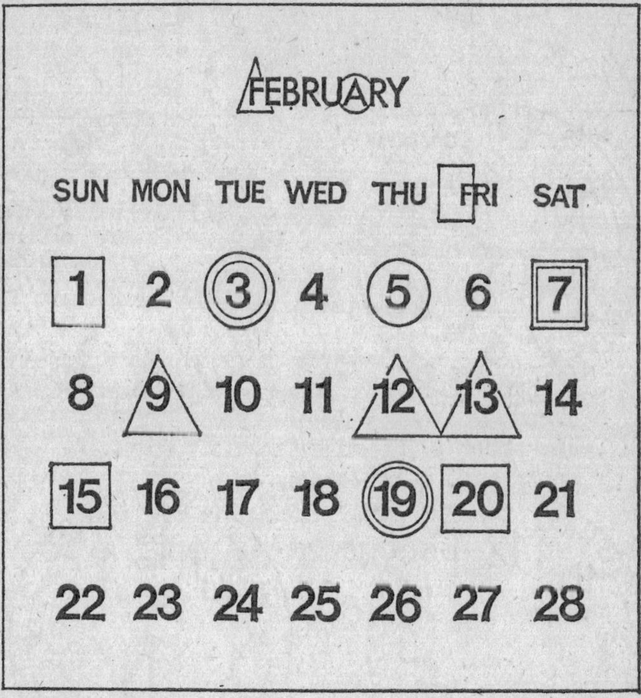

(B) WHAT WORD IS REPRESENTED BY THESE DATES:

6th 5th 2nd 18th 21st 1st 18th 25th ?

7. Where do the hands point at E?

A

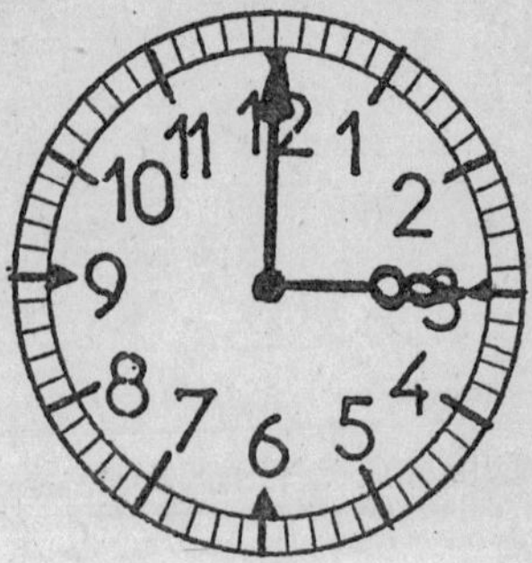

B

C

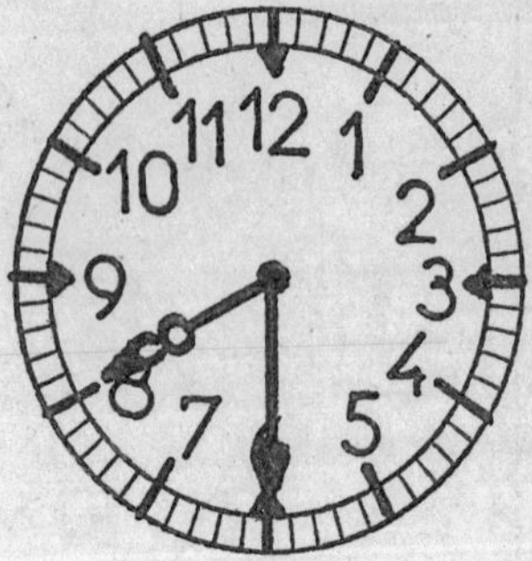

D

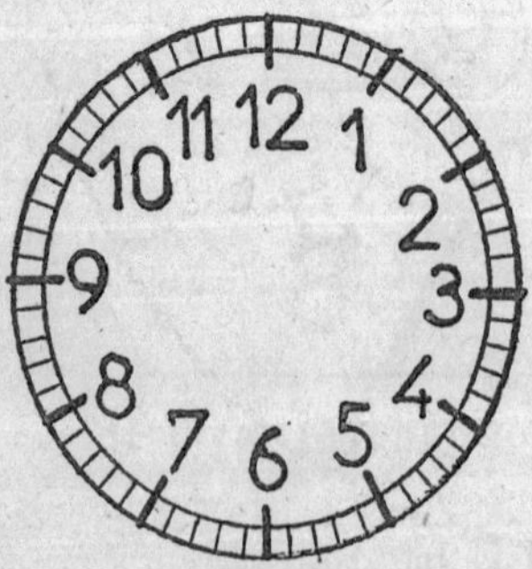

E

F

8. Complete this sequence:

G H N
H I M
J G K
N J H
\- - -

9. What is X?

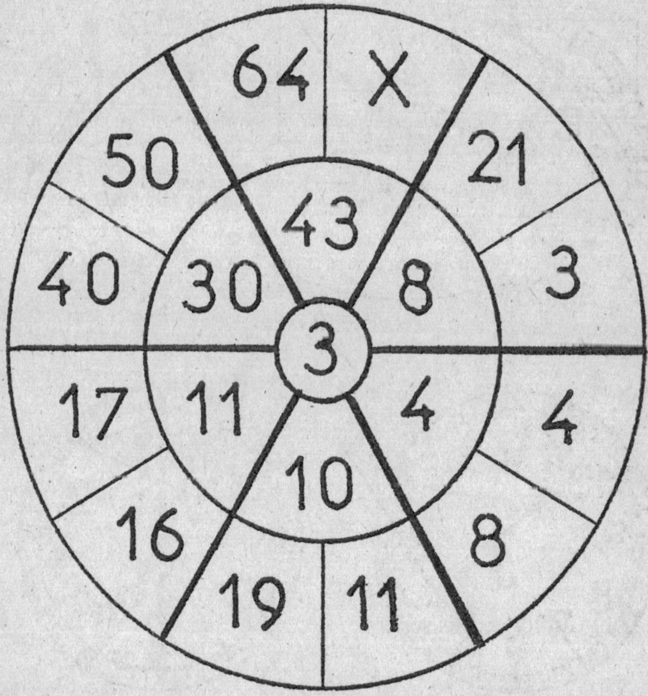

10. Which one does not conform?

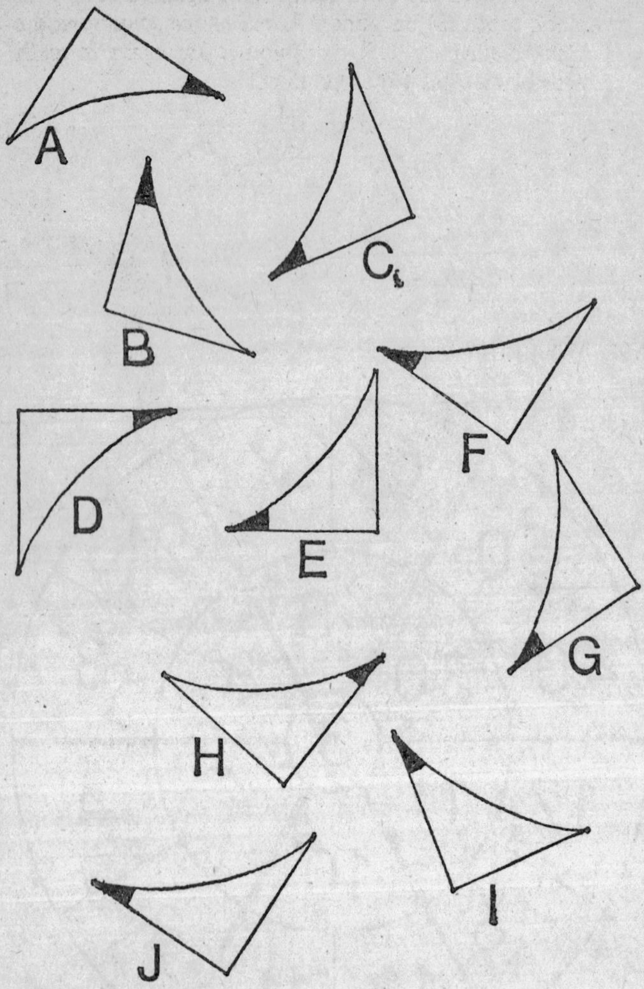

11. Complete this series:

1 2 3 7 8 9 28 29 30

_ _ _

12. How many revolutions of A will take place before the black teeth (1 and 2) on pinion B are again in mesh with black tooth (3) on pinion A *and at the same time* the black teeth (4 and 5) on pinion B are again in mesh with black tooth (6) on pinion C?

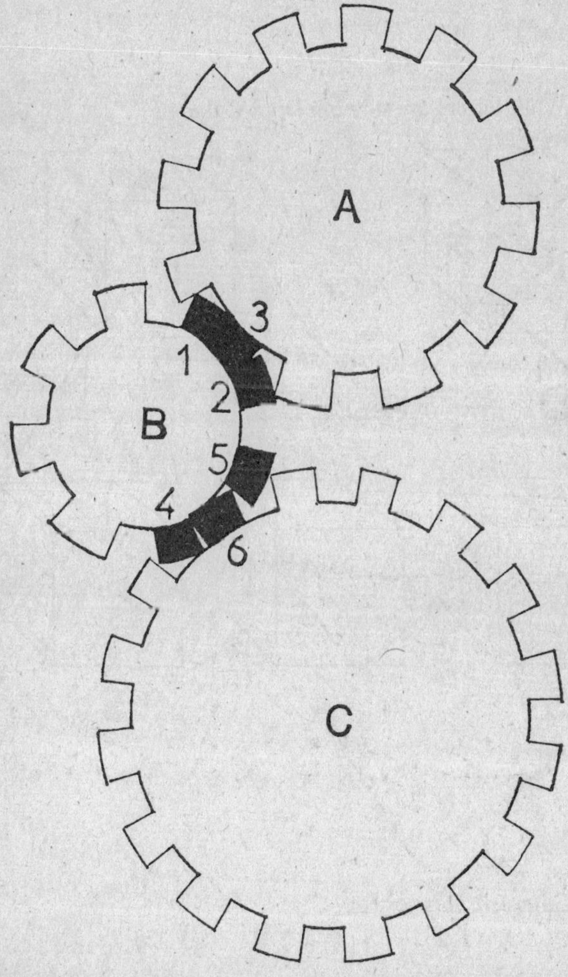

13. What letters are missing from Cube 4?

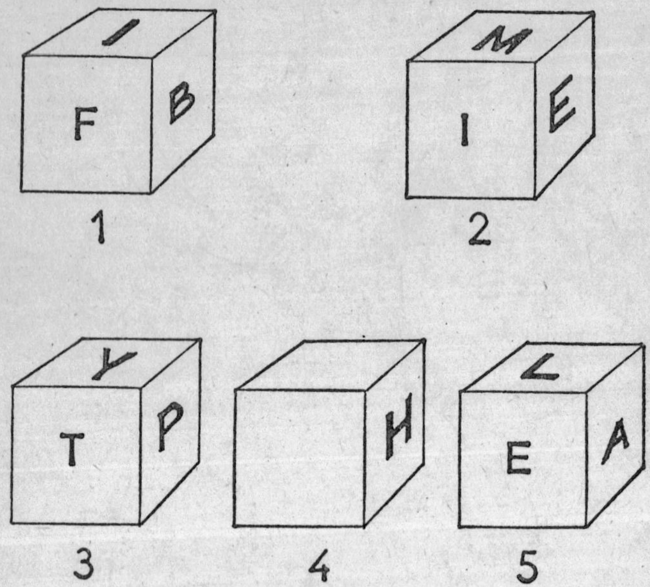

14. Which of the four figures at the bottom should follow No. 6?

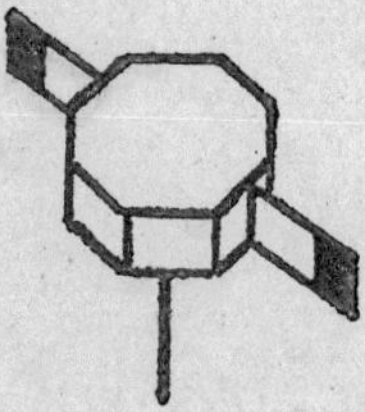

1

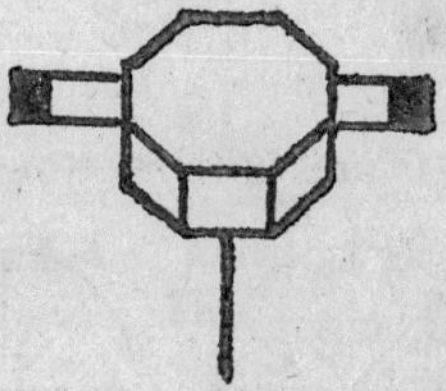

2

3

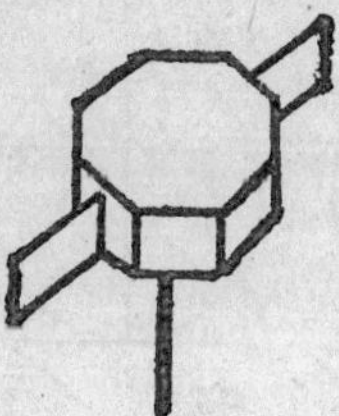

4

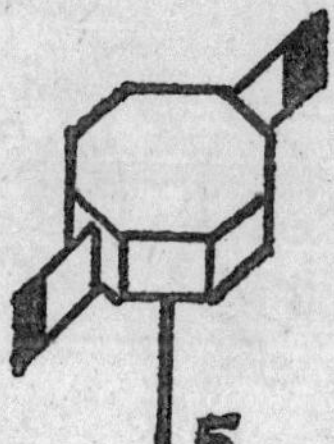

5

6

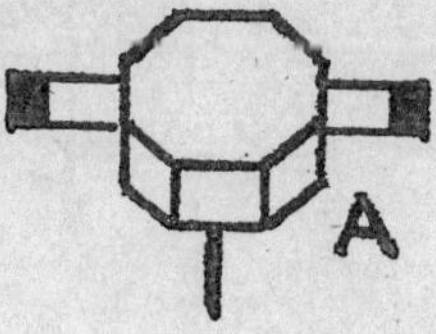

A

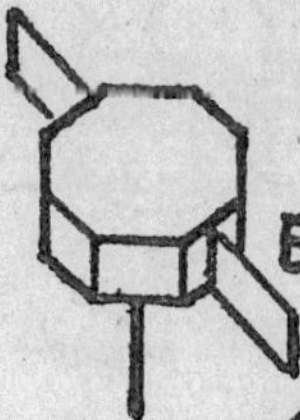

B

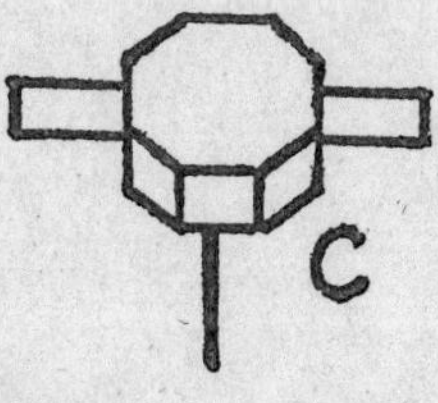

C

D

15. Which of the figures at the bottom belongs to No. 5?

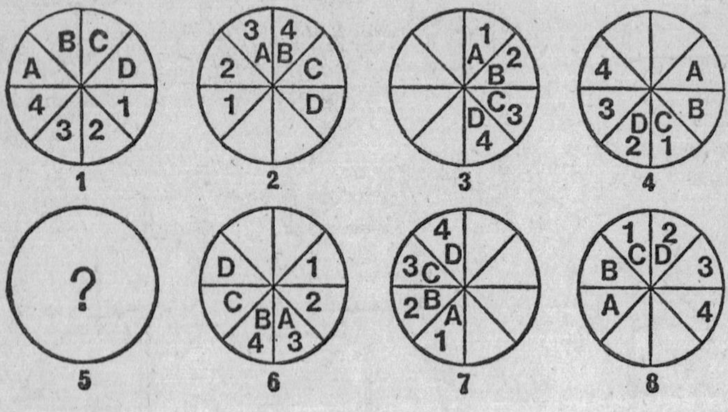

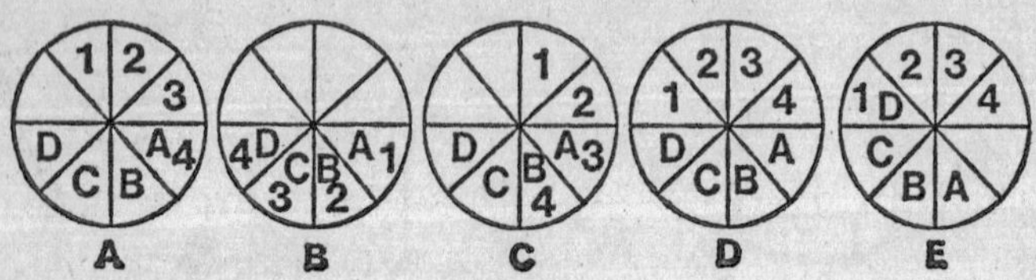

TEST No. 14

(Time limit: 75 minutes)

1.

MANTLE = 18

ZEAL = 12

EXTENT = 17

TENEMENT = ?

2. What completes the third circle?

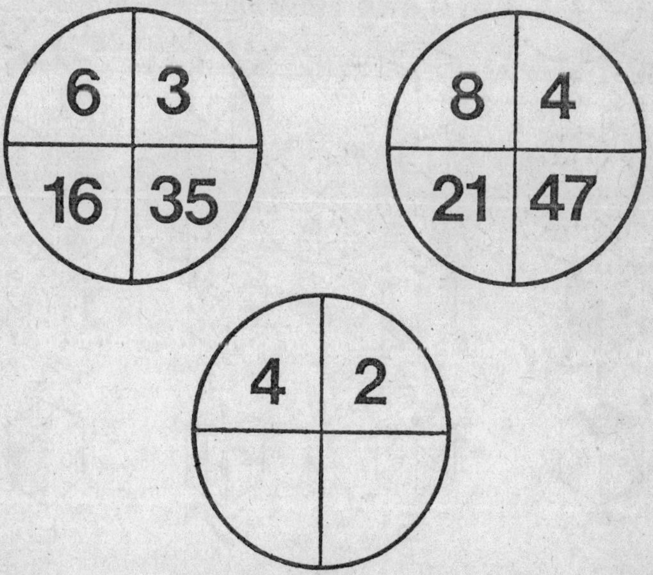

3. Which of the numbered cubes at the bottom belong to A, B, C and D?

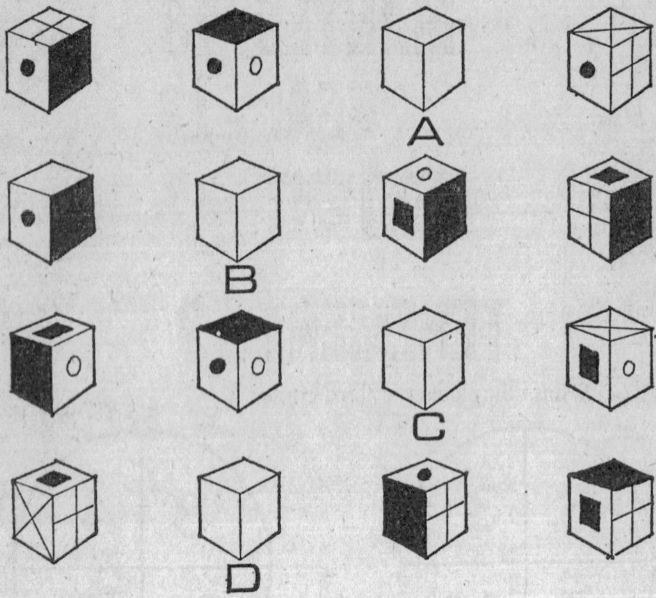

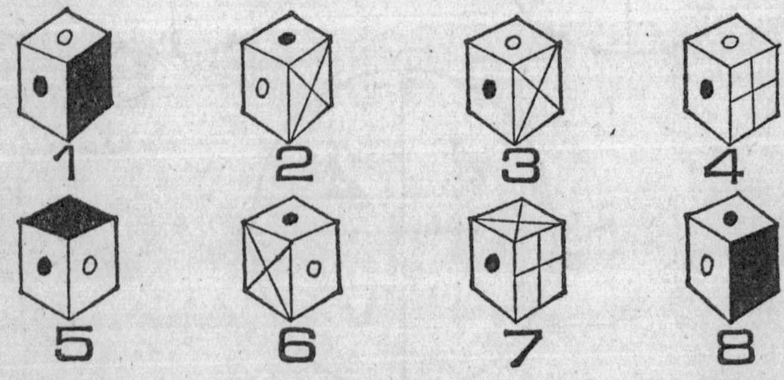

4. What animals are represented by A, B and C?

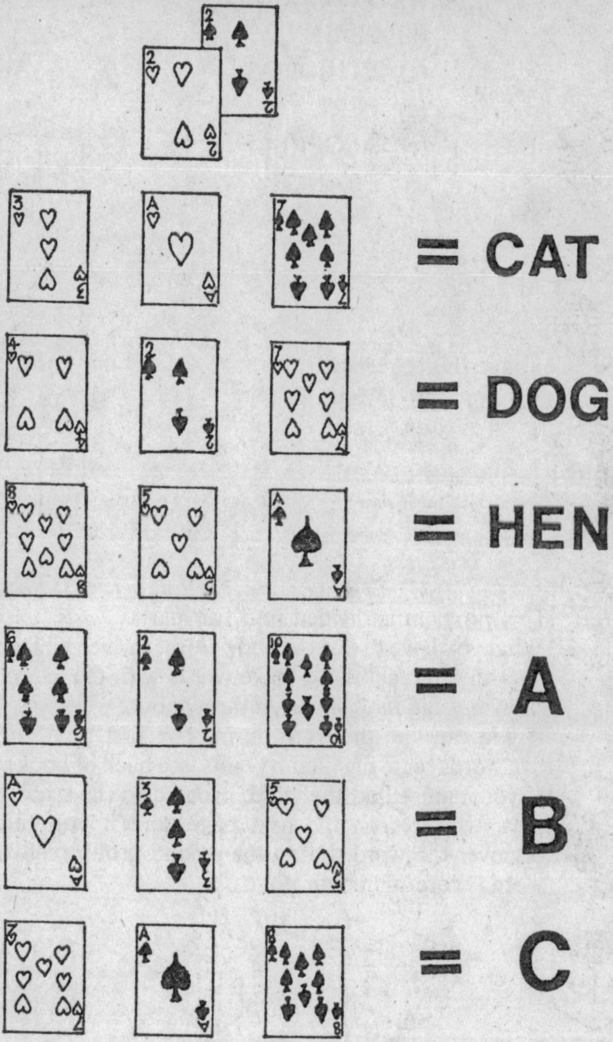

5. Which is the odd man out?

(a) VENEZUELA
(b) SPAIN
(c) ETHIOPIA
(d) PERU
(e) ALGERIA
(f) FRANCE

6. Continue this sequence:

b Q 17 e N 8 h K 11 k H 14 n

– – –

7(a) This problem is divided into two parts.
What you have to do is to find *one word* which will go into all the brackets to make words with the letters shown, using *the same word* throughout.
If you can find the word during this first group of five words score maximum points (see back of book).
If you cannot find the word, proceed to the second part, which is on the next page, and if you can discover the word during the second group of five words score minimum points.

( ) T
S ( )
( ) CH
LU ( )
( ) ING

7(b). Here is the second group of words:

TIE (   )
(   ) NACE
HAIR (   )
(   ) AFORE
TERRA (   )

8. Change R A I N into S N O W in nine moves, changing one letter at a time.

R A I N
1.
2.
3.
4.
5.
6.
7.
8.
9. S N O W

9. Supply the missing number:

35	36	40
21	18	20
14	9	10
7	14	–

10. Give ME the time!

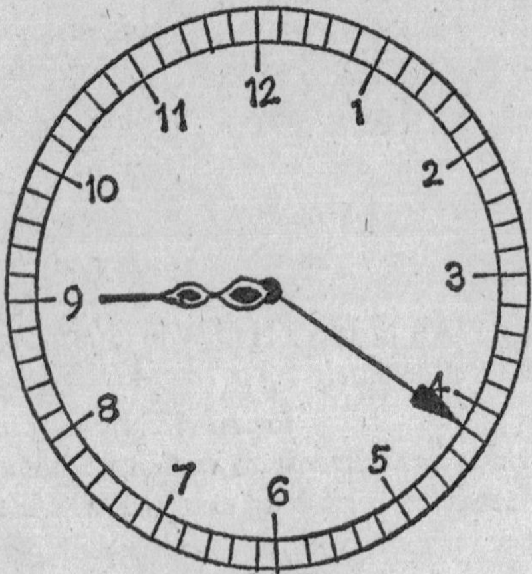

GO

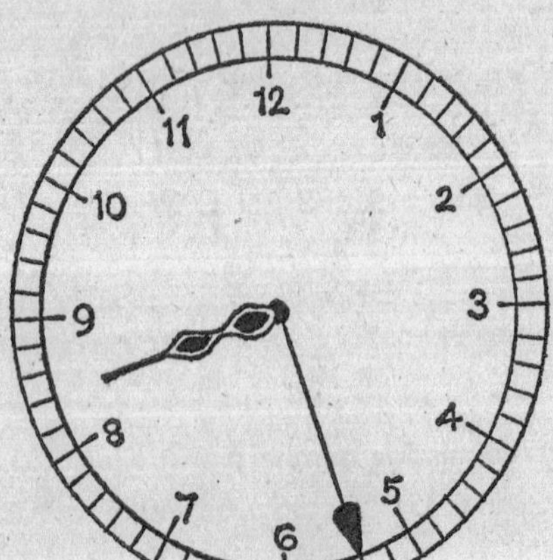

IN

11. Pair words in the first column with words in the second column.

HAM	SHOOTER
UNDER	CELLAR
SLEEP	BONE
LIGHT	MINE
LINE	PER
SHOP	SHIP
SHARP	GREEN
SALT	BURNER
PEA	PRACTICE
COAL	WALKER

12. Three poets are lurking in each of these sentences. Using each letter once only, can you find them?

1. TAKEN ABSURD FILMS, SEE?
2. THROW WORD ON SONNET, PEPYS.
3. O, END STORY IN DIRT – SMELT!

13. Find words which form a common link between the previous and the following word (for example: BOAT – *RACE* – HORSE).

COPPER

. . . . . .

GLASS

. . . . . .

HOLD

. . . . . .

CLEAR

. . . . . .

WARD

. . . . . .

SERVICE

14. Which of the letters at the bottom belong to a, b and c?

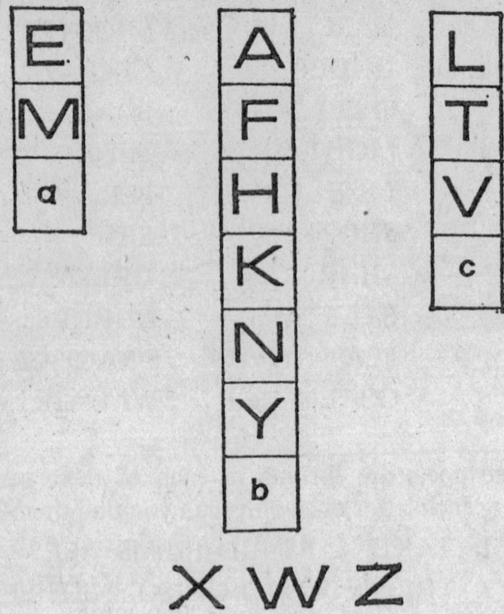

15. Which of the dice in the bottom row is SIX?

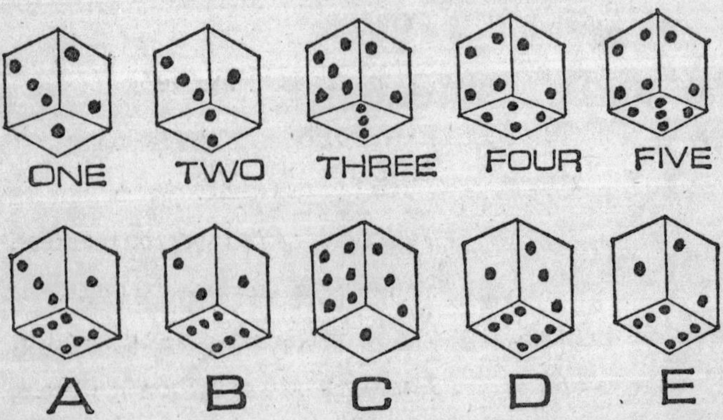

ANSWERS

TEST No. 11

1. No. 8.

The figure is rotated anti-clockwise throughout. Taking a unit as being a move of 45 degrees, in the first move (No. 2) it is turned one unit; then it is turned two units (No. 3). It is then successively turned 3, 4, 5, 6 and 7 units, bringing it to position No. 8. Therefore the next move will be eight units, in other words bringing it back to the same position as in position 8.
(Score 3 points)

2. 1 lb., 3 lbs., 9 lbs., 27 lbs.

The weights multiply by three progressively and the combined weight of all of them is 40 lbs.

If you worked it out by trial and error, it is obvious that there must be a weight of 1 lb. in order to weigh the smallest article. It would not be necessary to have a 2 lb. weight, since this could be achieved by putting a 3 lb. weight on one side of the scales and a 1 lb. weight on the other.

Individual weighings are made as follows:

2 lbs. ..... 3 on one side and 1 on the other.

4 lbs. ..... 3 and 1 on the same side.

5 lbs. ..... 9 on one side and 3 and 1 on the other.

6 lbs. ..... 9 on one side and 3 on the other.

7 lbs. ..... 9 and 1 on one side and 3 on the other.

8 lbs. ..... 9 on one side and 1 on the other,

and so on, eventually reaching 40 lbs., when all the weights are placed on one side only.
(Score 1 point for each correct weight. Maximum: 4 points)

3. No. 2.

The upper figures (in sharp keys) have open notes; the lower figures (in flat keys) have black notes.

The spacing between the notes is the same as the spacing between the sharps or flats. **(Score 2 points)**

4.

C A N I S T E R
S C A N S I O N
D E C A N T E R
D E S C A N T S
P E L I C A N S
A M E R I C A N

(Score 2 points, but only if all correct)

5. 36, 6.

Each alternate number is the square root of the one before it. The square roots progress in units – 3, 4 5 and 6.
(Score 1 point – but only if both correct)

6. 1.

Find the order in the alphabet of each letter of the words on each side of the brackets. The number in the brackets is the difference between the totals of these letters, thus:

C (3) + A (1) + T (20) = 24
D (4) + O (15) + G (7) = 26

The difference between 26 and 24 (2) is placed inside the brackets. **(Score 2 points)**

7. A = 8

B = 5

If an even number is at the top, add the three faces and then add the top number.
If an odd number is at the top, add the three faces and then subtract the top number.
Thus, in A, as there is an even number at the top, add the three faces: 3, 2 and 1, and add the top number (2), making a total of 8.
In B, as there is an odd number at the top, add the three faces: 3, 2 and 1, making a total of 6, from which subtract the top number (1), giving 5 as the result.
(Score 2 points for each correct. Maximum: 4 points)

8. (b), (c), (g), (h), (i). They should be spelt as follows: DESICCATE, ACCELERATE, INNUENDO, INOCULATE, IMPENETRABLE.

(Score 1 point for each word correct. Maximum: 5 points. *But deduct* 1 *point for each word you have wrongly chosen***)**

9. (e) APPLE, which begins and ends with a vowel. All the others begin and end with a consonant.
(Score 1 point)

10. $\frac{5}{25}$ in which the upper figure is the square root of the lower figure. In all the other fractions it is the cube root. **(Score 2 points)**

11. No. 2. The figure is rotating clockwise, a quarter-turn at a time.

Therefore, the fourth move at X will bring the black ends of the vanes into view again. **(Score 3 points)**

12. O L H 4 1 6 D.

From the previous number-plates it is fairly obvious that a code is used, and by referring to the letters D A F used in them it can be seen that D is represented by O (as in beDford and caDillac); A is represented by L (as in fiAT and cAdillac); F is represented by H (as in Fiat). The first three letters of the make of car is shown in code and the figures show the order in the alphabet of those same three letters. The year of registration for 1966 is D. **(Score 3 points)**

13. 63.

Each number is the square of the previous number minus one. **(2 points)**

14.

SEA-BED	(Black Sea and Bedclothes)
HORSESHOE	(Clothes-horse and Shoe horn)
BILLBOARD	(Hornbill and Board meeting)
PLACE-BET	(Meeting place and Betray)
ONWARD	(Rayon and Wardroom)

(Score 1 point for each correct link. Maximum: 5 points)

15. X = 144
Y = 400
Z = 256

The values of the shapes are as follows:

Square = 2

Triangle $= 4$
Rectangle $= 6$
Circle $= 8$

Where shapes overlap, add together the values of the individual shapes and square the result. Thus, in the examples given, where the circle and rectangle overlap the value is 196 $(6 + 8) = 14$. 14 squared $= 196$.

Where the triangle, rectangle and circle overlap the value is 324 $(4 + 6 + 8) = 18$. 18 squared $= 324$.
(Score 1 point for each. Maximum: 3 points)

TEST No. 12

1. WHEEL, BOY, MASTER, MEAL.
(Score 1 point for each link. Maximum: 4 points)

2. 315.

The number in each of the centre squares is the product minus the sum of the three numbers in the three corner squares surrounding it. Therefore, $8 \times 7 \times 6$, 336, minus $8 + 7 + 6$, $21 = 315$. **(2 points)**

3. The vicar would hardly know a month ahead that he had a funeral service to carry out. **(1 point)**

4. 256 11 5.

There are three series here, starting respectively with the first three numbers. The first sequence is 2, 4, 16 and 256 (each number is the square of the one before it); the second sequence is 2, 5, 8 and 11 (the numbers increase by three each time); the third sequence is

2, 3, 4 and 5 (numbers rising by one at a time).
(Score 2 points – but only if all correct)

5. CDLIX.

The progression is 51, 153, 459 and 1,377 (multiplying by three each time) expressed in Roman numerals.
(2 points)

6. PARSON, NOTICE, SPEARMINT, CHRISTMAS TREE, PINHEAD, OFFSIDE, ICE RINK, FOUNTAIN PEN, SONNET, HORSE BOX, CARROT.
(Score 1 point for each correct pair. Maximum: 11 points. ***But deduct 1 point for each incorrect pair*)**

7.

The symbols are made up of the letters B, C and D. In each case the letter is first printed the wrong way round and then the right way round, joining with a common line. The next term must be the letter 'E' made up in the same manner. **(2 points)**

8. 'ENEMY ATTACK EXPECTED TOMORROW.'

In the first word the letters in the message have been advanced one place in the alphabet.

In the second word they have been advanced two places.

In the third word they have been put one place back in their alphabetic order.

In the fourth word they have been put two places back. **(2 points – but only if all correct)**

9. E.

The figure is turned 45 degrees clockwise each time (the pointer in the circle indicates this), and the thick side is advanced one side on each move. E is wrong, therefore. Although the figure has turned 45 degrees clockwise the thick side has not been advanced at all. It *should* appear as follows:

(3 points)

10. 256 6,561 65,536.

There are three sequences here. In each case the first number is squared to give the next number. The sequences are: 2, 4, 16 (256); 3, 9, 81 (6,561); 4, 16, 256 (65,536). **(Score 2 points, but only if all correct)**

11. R S Q T P.

The letters across follow two series – ascending and descending alternately from the first letter. The letter commencing each row advances the letter that began the previous row by four places. **(2 points)**

12.

The top space indicates the vowels in the name as follows: A=1, E=2, I=3, O=4 and U=5. The bottom space indicates the number of consonants in the name. **(2 points)**

13.

A	C	R	E
R	E	E	L
I	R	I	S
D	E	N	E

(Score 2 points – but only if all correct)

14. 210.

After the first wicket had fallen 17 runs were added before the next wicket fell. Thereafter the additional runs scored were 15 (2 less), 19 (2 more), 13 (4 less), 21 (4 more), 11 (6 less), 23 (6 more), 9 (8 less) and finally 25 (8 more), making a grand total of 210 – thanks to the fine last wicket stand! **(3 points)**

15. 5.

There are three combined sequences here. Starting with the first number, the first sequence is: 1, 2, 3 and 4; the second number starts the next sequence of 7, 6, 5 and 4; the third number starts the third sequence of 3, 5 and 7. **(1 point)**

TEST No. 13

1. This is an old catch to which I have given a new dressing, strewing it with red herrings to put you off the scent of spotting the all-too-obvious answer.

In case you fell for any of the red herrings: December is midsummer in Durban, which is in the southern hemisphere; a stoep is a verandah found outside many houses in South Africa; the French Revolution was at its height in 1793; Robespierre executed many of his rival Girondins, and he himself was not executed until 1794.

No, the answer is really too easy!

How would we know what the lady was dreaming about if she was *killed instantly*?

(Score 1 point)

2. HALF A LOAF IS BETTER THAN NO BREAD.
(Score 1 point)

3. (a) The nine of diamonds;

   (b) The three of clubs;

   (c) The six of hearts;

   (d) The six of spades.

Red cards are for girls' names.
Black cards are for boys' names.
If a girl's name starts with a vowel the suit is diamonds.
If a girl's name starts with a consonant the suit is hearts.
If a boy's name starts with a vowel the suit is spades.
If a boy's name starts with a consonant the suit is clubs.
The number of pips is equal to the number of letters contained in the name.

(Score 2 points for each correct answer. Maximum: 8 points)

4.

The lower number indicates the number of *consecutive* letters in the world (aLMoner) and the upper number indicates the number of letters remaining.
(Score 3 points)

5. A. DAISY, ROSE, PEONY.

B. MARIGOLD, ANEMONE.

C. VIOLET, ROSEMARY.
(Score 1 point for each flower. Maximum: 7 points)

6. (A) FILM

(B) FEBRUARY

To solve (A) the first letter is taken from the letters in the headings, either the month or the days. Subsequent letters are shown by following the respective symbols. The dates show the order in the alphabet of the letters. Double letters are indicated by double symbols. Thus, following the triangles, F is the first letter (February); the second letter is indicated by 9 (I); the third letter by 12 (L) and the fourth letter by 13 (M).
To solve (B) simply take the dates given – 6, 5, 2, 18, 21, 1, 18 and 25 and substitute for them the letters of the same order in the alphabet.
(Score 3 points for A; 1 point for B. Maximum: 4 points)

7. The hour hand should point to 12 and the minute hand should point to 2. The hour hand advances progressively by 1 hour, 2 hours, 3 hours, *4 hours* and 5 hours. The minute hand advances by 5 minutes, 10 minutes, 20 minutes, *40 minutes* and 80 minutes. **(Score 4 points)**

8. V F D.

The letters in the first column advance their positions by 1, 2, 4 and 8 places (G – H – J – N – V); the letters in the middle column advance one place, then go back two places, then advance three places and finally go back 4 places (H – I – G – J – F); the letters in the right-hand column go back 1, 2, 3 and 4 places (N – M – K – H – D). **(Score 3 points)**

9. 65.

In each segment of the circle the two numbers in the outer ring are added and then divided by three (the common divisor indicated in the centre of the circle). The result is entered in the inner ring. **(2 points)**

10. H.

In all the others the black point is to the right of the right-angle. In H the black point is to the left of the right-angle. **(2 points)**

11. 121 122 123.

Each group of three consecutive numbers starts by first doubling the last number of the previous group and adding one (1 2 3 = 3 doubled + 1 = 7); then trebling the last number of the previous group and adding one (7 8 9 = 9 trebled + 1 = 28); finally quadrupling the last number of the previous group and adding one (28 29 30 = 30 multiplied by 4 + 1 = 121). **(2 points)**

12. 4 REVOLUTIONS. **(4 points)**

13.

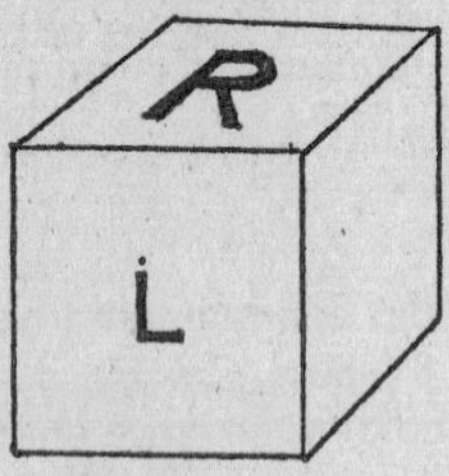

The letter on the left-hand bottom face of the cube advances that on the right-hand face by four places. The letter on the top face advances that on the bottom left-hand face by 3 places in 1, 4 places in 2, 5 places in 3, *six places in* 4, and 7 places in 5. **(Score 3 points)**

14. C.

The model is rotated anti-clockwise.
The first move is one face of the octagonal-shaped hub; the second two faces; the third three faces, and so on.
Therefore, after position 6 the vanes are rotated six faces, bringing them to the position shown in C.
(Score 3 points)

15. D.

Imagine that the circle consists of two semi-circles, each having independent movement from the other. The entire figure is rotated clockwise.
In each movement the semi-circle containing the letters – A, B, C and D moves forward by one segment. The semi-circle containing the numbers 1, 2, 3 and 4, moves forward *three* segments each time. **(Score 3 points)**

TEST No. 14

1. 26.

Add together the total number of strokes that make up the letters. (T = 2, E = 4, N = 3, E = 4, M = 4, E = 4, N = 3, T = 2.) **(Score 2 points)**

2.

Multiply the number in the top left-hand quarter by 6 and subtract 1. (4 multiplied by 6 = 24, less 1 = 23.) Multiply the number in the top right-hand quarter by 5 and add 1. (2 multiplied by 5 = 10, plus 1 = 11.) **(Score 1 point)**

3. A = 3

B = 8

C = 6

D = 7

In the top row across the cube is turned one face at a time, with the facing black spot remaining in the same position. It can be deduced that after the black face at the top (second cube) the next face visible at the top will have a white spot.
In the second row across the black side remains in position and the face with the black spot goes to the top. In each case the remaining face can be deduced by examining the other faces in the same row.
The third and fourth rows are changed in a similar way. **(Score 2 points for each correct answer. Maximum: 8 points)**

4. A = SOW

B = APE

C = GNU

The top cards denote the order of suits – hearts and spades.
The cards are numbered from 1 to 26, which numbers are substituted for the 26 letters of the alphabet.
Thus, in A: the six of spades is the 19th letter of the alphabet (S); the two of spades is the 15th letter (O); the ten of spades is the 23rd letter (W).
(Score 2 points for each correct animal. Maximum: 6 points)

5. (d) PERU, which is south of the Equator. All the other countries are north of the Equator. **(Score 2 points)**

6. E 5 q.

There are three sequences here.
The small letter (beginning with b) advances three places at a time – b, e, h, k, n, *q*.
The large letter (beginning with Q) goes back three places at a time – Q, N, K, H, *E*.
The numbers are the order in the alphabet of the letter preceding and following the numbers alternately (17 follows Q – the 17th letter; 8 precedes h – the 8th letter; 11 follows K – the 11th letter; 14 precedes n – the 14th letter; 5 follows E – the 5th letter).
(Score 3 points)

7. PIN.
(Score 5 points if you solved it in the first half, but only 1 point if solved in the second half. Maximum: 5 points)

8. R A I N

1. L A I N
2. L O I N
3. L O O N
4. B O O N
5. B O O T
6. B L O T
7. B L O W
8. S L O W
9. S N O W

(Score 3 points – but only if all correct)
(You may score maximum points if you used other words, provided they are genuine words)

9. 7 – so that each column adds up to 77.
(Score 2 points)

10.

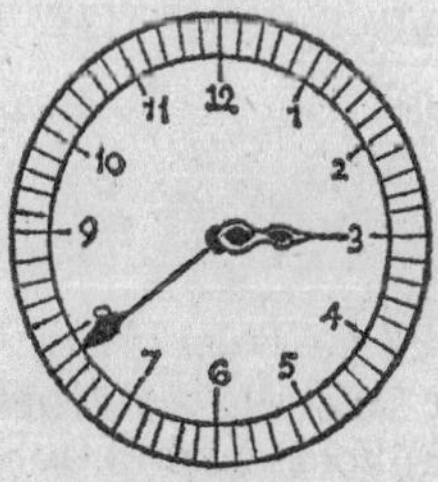

ME is 21 minutes to three (or 2.39). The hour hand should point towards 3 and the minute hand towards the 39th minute.
Three minutes passes for each letter of the alphabet.
Thus: A is 3 minutes, B is 6 minutes, and so on.
The minute hand indicates the first letter.
M is the 13th letter of the alphabet, so the hand points to the 39th minute.

The hour hand indicates the second letter, which is E. Being the 5th letter of the alphabet, the hand points to 15 minutes, i.e. 3 o'clock. **(Score 5 points)**

11. HAMBONE SHOPPER
UNDERMINE SHARP PRACTICE
SLEEPWALKER SALT CELLAR
LIGHTSHIP PEA GREEN
LINE SHOOTER COAL BURNER
(Score 1 point for each correct pair. Maximum: 10 points. But deduct one point for each incorrect pair)

12. 1. MASEFIELD, BURNS, KEATS.
2. WORDSWORTH, TENNYSON, POPE.
3. ROSSETTI, DRYDEN, MILTON.
(Score 1 point for each poet. Maximum: 9 points)

13. PLATE
HOUSE
ALL
WAY
ROOM

The links are as follows: copper (PLATE) glass; glass (HOUSE) hold; hold (ALL) clear; clear (WAY) ward; ward (ROOM) service.
(Score 1 point for each correct link. Maximum: 5 points)

14. a = W
b = Z
c = X

The first column consists of letters with four strokes;

the second column consists of letters with three strokes; the third column consists of letters with two strokes.
(Score 1 point for each correct answer. Maximum: 3 points)

15. A

The bottom face indicates the actual number (six).
The left-hand face shows the number of letters in the word (one = 3, two = 3; three = 5, four = 4, five = 4, six = 3).
The right-hand face shows the number of vowels in the word (OnE = 2, twO = 1, thrEE = 2, fOUr = 2, fIvE = 2, sIx = 1).
(Score 2 points)

GROUP III

Ratings for Tests 11–14

The total score possible for these four tests is: 199, made up as follows:

TEST No. 11	42 points
TEST No. 12	41 points
TEST No. 13	50 points
TEST No. 14	66 points

Points are only scored for answers given within the specified time limits.

This was an extremely difficult group, but take heart from the fact that a score as low as **90–100** is 'average'.

The majority of the points were scored by logical reasoning and deduction; so if you scored unusually low points it is likely that you have acquired the technique of working out problems of a numerical or spatial nature but could improve at trying to regard things from a less straightforward attitude. Or perhaps, once again, time defeated you more than the problems themselves.

Therefore, if you scored over 100 you should feel well pleased with your reasoning powers.

150 and over is so excellent that you should never again be afraid to tackle any type of test of this nature. In view of what I wrote in the introduction you had better not claim to having superior intelligence, but could certainly claim that you understand this type of test and can fathom what is in the mind of the inquisitor.

Although under 90 is below average, the tests were so difficult that if you have a score of 75–90 you have nothing to be ashamed of.

Below 75 I can only express the hope that you enjoyed trying to unravel the problems as much as I enjoyed setting them, and I trust I haven't taxed your brain too much!

Non-fiction in Tandem editions

Name ....

Address ....

Titles required.................................

....

....

....

....

....

....

- - - - - - - - - - - - - - - - - -

The publishers hope that you enjoyed this book and invite you to write for the full list of Tandem titles.

If you find any difficulty in obtaining these books from your usual retailer we shall be pleased to supply the titles of your choice upon receipt of your remittance.

Packing and postage charges are as follows:

U.K. One book 18p plus 8p per copy for each additional book ordered to a maximum charge of 66p.

B.F.P.O. and Eire 18p for the first book plus 8p per copy for the next 6 books, thereafter 3p per book.

WRITE NOW TO:

Tandem Publishing Ltd.,
14 Gloucester Road,
London SW7 4RD

A Howard & Wyndham Company

While every effort is made to keep prices low, it is sometimes necessary to increase prices at short notice. Tandem Books reserve the right to show new retail prices on covers which may differ from those previously advertised in the text or elsewhere.